Uttamapuruṣa:

reflections on the process of meditation

Uttamapuruṣa:
reflections on the process of meditation

Carlos Eduardo Gonzales Barbosa

Translated by

Joana Allis

Uttamapuruṣa:
reflections on the process of meditation
Carlos Eduardo Gonzales Barbosa

1st English Edition: October 2022

Translated from the original:
'Uttamapuruṣa: reflexões sobre o processo da meditação'

© of the translation: Joana Allis

ISBN: 978-65-991900-6-3

Cataloging-In-Publication (CIP)
(eDOC BRASIL)

B238u Barbosa, Carlos Eduardo Gonzales, 1957-.
Uttamapuruṣa: reflections on the process of meditation / Carlos Eduardo Gonzales Barbosa. – Florianópolis, SC: Yogaforum.org, 2022.
170 p. : 16 x 23 cm

Includes bibliography
Título original: Uttamapuruṣa: reflexões sobre o processo da...
ISBN 978-65-991900-6-3

1. Hinduism. 2. Meditation. 3. Yoga. I. Title.

DDC 294.543

Prepared by Maurício Amormino Júnior – CRB6/2422

Table of Contents

Preface

This is the first book in which I write exclusively about the process of meditation. These twenty chapters are organized from reflections that were originally independent notes. When I started writing, still somewhat skeptical about the value of the information I had gathered to share, I realized that there was consistent coherence throughout the texts I was working with. The through-line between the various writings was found in the word 'Puruṣa' with its remarkable pendular semantics, alternating between the 'cosmic man' of the Vedas, the grammatical verbal first-person and the higher self that inhabits the heart of all creatures. The search for an internal connection of the mind with Puruṣa is the guiding thread of our journey through the universe of meditation.

Despite the rich parallels that can be drawn between the various perspectives of meditation across different cultures of Asia, I have only examined Hindu sources in this book. As such, this book is based solely on Sanskrit or Vedic Hindu culture. Even so, due to the vastness and richness of these sources, thousands of Sanskrit verses were read over and over to select the most enlightening sections to be cited here.

I should let the reader know that I do not reference Sanskrit translations, because, as high quality as they may be, I prefer to translate directly from the original text into Portuguese. The Portuguese text was then translated into English. This means that the translations you find here may have slight differences from other translations, some that are held in high esteem among academics and Sanskritists. In any case, I prefer to present a contextualized understanding of what the text is trying to say, without giving attention to opposing opinions. As an example, the expression 'Puruṣārthās' is frequently used to refer to the four goals of human life (dharma, artha, kāma and mokṣa), but it sometimes needs to be translated as 'meanings of Puruṣa' or 'interests of the higher self' in order to make sense in the sentence.

I am also aware that there are distinct differences between the various doctrines that I consulted to produce this text that is presented here. But the process of meditation is a field of knowledge that is capable of reconciling with relative ease those differences that would appear to divide the Sanātana Dharma into doctrinal theses that disagree with each other. Yoga, Sāṁkhya, Vedānta, epics, purāṇas and the Upaniṣads are some of the doctrines that came from the same cultural base, and they have a lot to offer one another and much to gain from the exchange of insights found within each one.

To facilitate the reader's understanding, I chose to use the transliteration of the Sanskrit terms using the IAST (International Alphabet of Sanskrit Transliteration) standard that has been used for over a century as the academic standard to represent the Devanāgarī alphabet.

The intention of this book is to give the reader an understanding of how meditation works from a Hindu perspective, as explained in ancient texts. In order to maintain focus on the process itself, references to techniques that are used to meditate have been removed. To learn more about the innumerable meditation techniques, it is recommended that the reader consult specialized texts about these techniques. Studying the process will make it possible to obtain much better results with any of the techniques that one chooses to use.

My hope is that the reflections that make up this book will help the reader to make the best use of the references that have been selected here, produced by very wise people from centuries past.

Carlos Eduardo Barbosa
Florianópolis, SC - Brazil
August 5, 2020

1. Introduction

Those who seek meditation generally do so with the hope of finding a tool or formula that, once put into practice, will create simple transformations, for the better, in their physical and mental health. Of course, there is good reason for this hope. There is much research that proves, with scientific rigor, the various benefits brought about by the practice of meditation.

These studies often show some of the more popular images of meditation, such as sitting in a comfortable position, relaxing the body, calming the mind, focusing on a defined object (like the breath, for example) or emptying the mind of thoughts. This suggests that such research is robust proof that meditation does indeed work.

This line of thought leads to the natural conclusion that there is a scientifically applicable, impersonal meditation technique - a meditation 'approved' by science. Supposedly, this technique, although derived from Eastern religious practices, could offer statistically predictable results according to some scientific theory. This result would be obtained relatively independently from possible subjective adverse conditions found in the person practicing them. Meditation would have the ability to provide resources to reduce or eliminate these adverse conditions. The growing acceptance of meditation in the scientific world is one of the reasons why it has become more common for doctors and psychologists to recommend it as a complementary therapy to their work.

The positive image of meditation is due in large part to its strong visibility. Scientific experiments have been carried out for decades to evaluate neurological development and changes in metabolism or in muscle tone of meditators. We can trace the history of these experiments back to 1924, in

India, starting with the work of the Kaivalyadhāma Yoga Institute and Research Center created by Swāmi Kuvalayānanda to promote scientific studies on yoga. More recently, studies of Tibetan Buddhist meditators conducted by Dr. Richard Davidson of the University of Wisconsin, Madison have gained acclaim. These studies have counted on the participation of Tibetan Buddhist meditators, chosen among the best by the Dalai Lama himself. This research has given more validity and strength to the theory of neuroplasticity, which has changed the scientific view of the dynamics of the tissues of the human nervous system.

Research like this is only possible because meditation involves internal processes of the human organism that can be studied objectively. And these processes can be reported respecting the indispensable scientific principle of objectivity in these studies. This impersonal objectivity (or lack of subjectivity) allows the researcher to describe experiments and results using, by default, the third-person in their writing. This impersonal format is needed in order to be in alignment with scientific methodology. Using this format correctly increases the respectability of the theses and strengthens scientific rigor. Scientific rigor alone offers credibility to research in any field and, can financially boost an academic career. Meditation has been scientifically studied by researchers of the most varied specializations, in all regions of the world. And the field of knowledge that opens up for anyone dedicated to researching meditation is still far from being exhausted.

But methodological limitations make it difficult for science to access certain less objective aspects of the experience of meditation. The detachment of science from the personal, from the individual, forces the researcher to construct a paradoxical form of knowledge, which, on the one hand originates from irrational human curiosity, and, on the other hand, rejects its undeniable connection with the individual, personal and subjective aspects of being human, that is, personhood. Scientific knowledge seeks a 'dehumanized' form of understanding, one that is not dependent on the individuals involved, and, therefore, does not recognize its dependence on the subjectivity of the human beings who created it.

If limits are not posed, the impersonality of science closes the door to scientific inquiry into certain areas of knowledge that can only be reached through a more personal, individualized and subjective lens, one that acknowledges personhood. Subjective information can be very useful to clarify topics such as the nature of consciousness, for example, a topic for which researchers have had much difficulty in accessing and describing through scientific theory. The Australian philosopher David Chalmers, when evaluating the conditions necessary for the progress of the science of consciousness, said the following:

"The task of a science of consciousness, as I see it, is to systematically integrate two key classes of data into a scientific framework: third-person data, or data about behavior and brain processes, and first-person data, or data about subjective experience. When a conscious system is observed from the third-person point of view, a range of specific behavioral and neural phenomena present themselves. When a conscious system is observed from the first-person point of view, a range of specific subjective phenomena present themselves. Both sorts of phenomena have the status of data for a science of consciousness." [1]

Chalmers' assertion is valid and accurate when considering the development of a science of meditation, because research in this area needs to consider topics such as consciousness, nature of the mind and free will, to name just a few. These are themes that require investigation that dares to advance into the subjective aspects of human life in order to be understood. The impersonal aspects of scientific research require more than just its reporting to be written in the third-person; the entire logic of the research is restricted to the third-person perspective. This significantly limits the possibility of collecting and including data that depends in any way on the subjectivity of the first-person. This, in the study of meditation, restricts the field of study to measurable aspects, such as its effects on health, limiting the results to an area that is actually the least important for the meditator, that is, according to literary sources from past millennia, which describe what is considered to be the original meditation.

Another aspect of the impersonality of science to be considered here is the understandable need to leave out any data produced by personal opinions of the researcher as well as of a person being studied. For the sake of the research, both need to be impersonalized, the study needs to focus on universal characteristics of those involved. Whatever the personal beliefs of the researcher or research subject may be, they will be ignored unless they are an integral part of the research scope. The impersonality of the construction of science may also end up negatively interfering in the

---

[1] Chalmers, David J. The Character of Consciousness (Philosophy of Mind) (p. 37). Oxford University Press. Kindle edition.

professional relationship of therapists (doctors, psychologists, physiotherapists, and others) with their patients.

In the 1950's, a North American psychotherapist named Carl Rogers came to notice how harmful impersonality could become over the course of our lives and within relationships between human beings. His assessment, from both the therapist's and the patient's point of view, was that the effort put into being impersonal carries the risk of making the individual increasingly false and less capable. Rogers, in his best-known work, "On Becoming a Person," presents some reflections on this topic. He says:

> *"In my relationships with persons I have found that it does not help, in the long run, to act as though I were something that I am not."* [2] *(...) "the curious paradox is that when I accept myself as I am, then I change. (...) we cannot change, we cannot move away from what we are, until we thoroughly accept what we are. Then change seems to come about almost unnoticed."* [3]

Rogers is referring to a change in mental state, that is, a subjective change that is made possible through the perception and conscious acceptance of one's own personhood. For Rogers, the challenge is to understand who the person is that he is interacting with, so that helping that person becomes possible. Rogers says:

> *"I have found it of enormous value when I can permit myself to understand another person. (...) Even more important perhaps, is the fact that my understanding of these individuals permits them to change."* [4]

Carl Rogers became a voice that resonated throughout the counterculture movement of the 1960's, signaling the importance of 'becoming a person' for better results in the practical application of rigorously scientific theories.

Psychology, as with other areas of scientific study, has strong roots in philosophy, a subject whose importance cannot be minimized. Meditation is also a field of knowledge that has both a scientific and a philosophical side, if not more. The practice of meditation comes entirely from its philosophical base and is filled with subjectivity. In some aspects, meditation

---

[2] ROGERS, Carl R. On Becoming a Person (p. 16). Little, Brown Book Group. Kindle edition.

[3] Idem, p.17.

[4] Idem, p.18-19.

can be confused with mystical or religious practices. Only a small portion of these practices involve activities of the body that can result in measurable changes in the physiology of the practitioner, which, in turn, produce objective information that can be observed through scientific method.

The large number of scientific studies about meditation clearly shows the importance that this topic has gained on a global scale. We have such admiration and respect for the effort put in by each one of these researchers in their quest to comprehend the wide-ranging impact that meditation has on the health of its practitioners. We certainly know more and more about this with each passing day, as the number of new scientific studies about this topic only grows.

Philosophy, specifically philosophy of the mind, is another area that could make a great contribution to the conversation about meditation. Our journey into the process of meditation will be conducted using this path of philosophy, but from the point of view of a more ancient philosophy, of course. More specifically, we will explore the philosophy of Sāṁkhya and yoga, through the Upaniṣads and Tantra, considered to be the main sources of information regarding the origin and nature of the process of meditation. All of the literary sources that we are going to consult are written in Vedic dialects or Sanskrit, languages spoken in ancient India. The literary texts which we will focus on throughout these reflections are already known to students and practitioners of yoga and Vedanta, although their understanding may be slightly different from what will be presented here in this book.

With all of this in mind, we will leave the production of scientific studies to the scientists, and we will focus on a kind of archeology of the process of meditation. We will be analyzing this process in its original form, as presented by its oldest known proponents - the poets of the Vedic-Sanskrit culture.

You may be surprised by how much modernity can be found in these ancient Indian texts...

2. What is meditation?

Sometimes we study a subject for a long time without understanding what it actually has to teach us. Not because of lack of attention or care in researching the information, but because the mind, at some point along the way, has been caught up by an incorrect understanding. Contaminated by our attachment to this piece of incorrect information, the mind is impaired in its discernment. It is extremely difficult to learn more about a topic that one believes they have already mastered, that is, for which the mind has lost its most important characteristic: freedom.

In order to give the mind back that lost freedom, the best thing to do is to allow for unbiased reflection on the thing you hope to understand more deeply. It is suggested that the first step in this reflection is the most basic of all: clarifying the word used to name the subject. Although at first glance, this can seem unnecessary, one might be surprised by the information that can be found through simply leafing through a dictionary and looking for the meaning and etymology of words that were supposedly already known. Hence the question asked in the title of this chapter: what is 'meditation'?

'Meditation' is an act, the act of meditating. The verb 'meditate' comes from the word 'meditor' in Latin, which means to exercise, prepare, study or do. In turn, the verb 'meditor' is derived from the older verb 'medeor' that means to treat, care for, medicate, cure or take measures. The word 'meditation' in Latin is 'meditatio' which means preparation, exercise, practice, study or work. The Greek equivalent to 'meditatio' is 'meléte' (μελέτη), which has the same meanings. Meditation was understood, in ancient times, as an exercise, a practice or a preparation, that is, a disciplined action produced with the body or the mind. According to this original, older meaning, the student dedicated to research, or the athlete dedicated to the practice of weight-training are equally meditators. Over time, however, the word 'meditation' evolved to mean the action of contemplating with the mind. This is the meaning that we give to meditation today: an essentially subjective action, carried out through the mind, but, still a practice, an exercise.

Ancient Sanskrit literature generally follows the same pattern as Latin and Greek. The two sustaining pillars of meditation, according to the yoga doctrine are continued practice (*abhyāsa*) and detachment (*vairāgyam*). It seems that there was consensus in ancient Europe and Asia about the practical nature of meditation. Meditation is exercising, it's practicing, it is doing something with discipline. Meditation, according to Sanskrit culture, is the act of putting into practice an internal mental process that will help the practitioner adopt and maintain a special attitude towards one's own self - an attitude of freedom.

Within the territory of the Indian subcontinent, various techniques that lead to meditation were born, but the internal process that each of these mobilize is just one, and the same one. Meditation itself is the subjective process that seeks to free the 'I', or the 'self', from the oppression of the 'other.' A process that removes the self from the condition of passivity and puts this self in the position of command over one's own life. This process involves actions that take place, in large part, in the realms of the mind that are meant to strengthen the presence of this internal 'self' in one's life. This idea can be summarized by saying that meditation is the continued exercise of the meditator's unique and personal nature. Or, to put it more simply, meditation is the process by which a practitioner can discover their best self (their authentic nature) and put this version of self into practice.

The process of meditation that has spread throughout South Asia is universally applicable. It is carried out using the natural resources found within every human being. It is necessary, however, to find these resources and put them to use in order to enjoy their benefits. Finding these subjective resources and exercising their functionality are the primary tasks of the process of meditation. It is now time for us to explore the Sanskrit terms for 'meditation' so that we can extract from them a better understanding of what meditation meant in ancient India.

Among the oldest Vedic nouns that mean 'meditation' are '*dhī*' and '*dhyā*,' both of which express intense attention or solemn thought. Both have existed for over four thousand years and come from the verb '*dhā*' (or '*dhi*,' the weaker form of the same verb), which means 'to place,' and was often used to construct subjective expressions such as 'to place attention' or 'to place (offer) an opinion.' These Vedic words are the root for the Sanskrit verb '*dhyai*,' which means to think, imagine, contemplate, reflect, or, in a word, to meditate. According to Hindu Dharma, the actions expressed by this verb are found in the mind or in the heart. From the verbal root '*dhyai*' came the Sanskrit word most used to this day to mean 'meditation': '*dhyānam*.' When the prefix '*ni*' is added, which means 'inward,' the verb '*dhyai*' produces the Sanskrit words '*nidhyapti*' and '*nididhyāsanam*,' both of which represent a deeper, more repetitive meditation.

In parallel to the evolution of the word '*dhyānam*', the Vedic verb '*dhā*' evolved to be accompanied by two prefixes ('*sam*' and '*ā*') to form the verb '*sam-ā-dhā*' ('to bring together,' 'to add') which gradually gets closer to the meaning of 'to meditate.' This development is revealed through the expression '*samādhānam kṛ*' ('to pay attention'). But the noun '*samādhi*,' among the derivatives of the verb '*sam-ā-dhā*' ('*dhi*' in its weaker form), is the word that comes closest to the original concept of meditation.

'*Samādhi*' approaches two other Vedic words born from the same root verb '*yuj*' ('to harness,' 'to adjust'): '*yojanam*' and '*yoga*.' The semantic similarity between the word samādhi and these two other words leads Vyāsa to assert in his commentary on Patañjali's Yoga Sūtras that "*samādhi is yoga*"[5]. But, for Patañjali, this is only true in the sense that samādhi is an integral part of the meditation process. Patañjali differentiates the two words (samādhi and yoga) and gives a new meaning to the word for meditation, calling it '*saṁyama*.' This new name brings together three components - dhāraṇā, dhyānam and samādhi - in an integrated way, thus establishing the inner core of the method of yoga.

Constructed from the word '*yama*', which primarily means 'control', saṁyama is translated as 'joint control.' It is applied in the sense of joint control of the mind and senses. But, saṁyama also has other meanings. It can be used to describe a bun at the top of the head, an image that is often associated with those who meditate. Patañjali was prudent and conservative in using the older terms, dhyānam and samādhi, which were already established as terms used to mean meditation, but he innovated the use of these words by integrating them with the concept of sustainability, with the word dhāraṇā. This word comes from the root verb '*dhṛ*' ('to sustain'),

---

[5] Yoga Sūtra Bhāṣya, 1.1

the same one that gives rise to the word dharma - 'that which provides sustenance.' He gives this new meditation (saṁyama) the task of being sustained within the higher self ('*ātmā*'), which was previously a task attributed only to samādhi, as noted in the expression:

"All of this (the whole world) is recoiled (samāhitaṁ[6]) within the force of Brahma." [7]

Although there are many variations of the words for meditation in Sanskrit vocabulary, the most utilized word for meditation in Sanskrit is still 'dhyānam.' Throughout the centuries of development of the yoga doctrine, this word has held onto its past dignity, having received from Patañjali a special emphasis in the description of the process of meditation. The importance of this word in yoga will be discussed in a later chapter. For now, we will return to the discussion of personhood - of the personal, individual and subjective - in meditation, the topic of the next chapter.

---

[6] Past participle of the verb samādhā, which gives rise to the word 'samādhi.'
[7] Chāndogya Upaniṣad 8.1.4

3. Personhood in Meditation

Sanskrit culture is generally uninterested in the idea of the principle of impersonality or impartiality. However, many Indian academics defend the idea that the Sanskrit language is perfect for developing scientific texts. This claim is due to the rigorous structure of its grammar and the richness of its vocabulary, qualities that are needed to compose texts that require precision. It is true that this precision can be found in ancient Sanskrit texts that discuss mathematics or astronomy, for example. But, even these texts, which may appear to be scientific in character, are filled with a subjectivity that Sanskrit culture sees in the substance of numbers, words and physical matter. Numbers, words and matter are considered to be signs that point to a subjective presence to which the creation of the universe is attributed. This presence is called, in Sanskrit, by the masculine name 'Puruṣa', the universal person.

Using Puruṣa as an example, let us take a brief tour of Sanskrit literature in order to find some clarity about this principle of personhood that we are referring to. Let's start with a small excerpt from a great epic.

The longest epic in the world was composed in Sanskrit and is called Mahābhāratam. Through its 85,000+ double verses, the epic narrates a sequence of tragic events that occur in a mythical royal family (the Lunar Dynasty) divided in two opposing groups vying for power through a great war. The text itself claims its author to be the mythical sage Kṛṣṇa Dvaipāyana Vyāsa Deva, a member of the Lunar Dynasty and a key character in the epic's plot. Over time, the main narrative was added to with independent texts, most of them instructive. One of these texts is a brief dialogue [8] between the god Brahmā and his son Rudra where they discuss Puruṣa:

> *"(...) In the middle of the Ocean of Milk, there is a high mountain, which is shiny like gold, called Vaijayanta, where the throne of the sovereign lies (virāj). There sits a solitary god, thinking about the path that leads to the higher self (ātmā). Then Śiva arrives, the god born from the forehead of the four-faced sage (Brahmā). Overcome with affection, he offered homage at the feet of Brahmā, who, with his left hand made him rise and said:*
>
> *"Welcome! I am glad that you have come to me. How is everything, my son? Are you still committed to proper study and purification practices?*
>
> *"Rudra says:*
>
> *"By the grace that comes from thee, o Bhagavān, my studies and purifications are excellent and unshakable, like everything else in the universe! For a long time, I have seen Bhagavān on the sovereign's throne, which is why I came here to meet him. I'm curious to know the reason, which can't be insignificant, for coming to this lonely place. Why, having a better throne, free from hunger and thirst, frequented by Suras, Asuras, by brilliant sages, by singers and celestial nymphs, did you still come here to stand alone?*
>
> *" Brahmā says:*
>
> *"I am permanently on this desirable mountain Vaijayanta. Here, with my mind focused, I think of the sovereign Puruṣa."*

Before continuing with the story, it is important to clarify that the word 'Puruṣa' is used in Sanskrit to mean 'man' (a masculine gendered person) as well as an abstract 'person' without gender, who is not necessarily a human person. Although there are other words that could be translated to 'person,' this was the one chosen by the ancient sages of India to identify the presence of 'personhood' within philosophical thought. Therefore, we will often use the word 'person' when translating the term 'Puruṣa.' And now back to the story:

---

[8] Chapters 12-338 and 12-339 of the BORI critique edition, corresponding to chapters 12-350 and 12-351 of the Parimal edition.

"Rudra says:

"Many people were created by you, Brahmā, who arose from you your-self, when that unique and sovereign person already existed. Who is this supreme person (Puruṣottama) you think of? Answer this question for me. My curiosity is great.

"Brahmā says:

"Many are the people you mention, my son. Still, though invisible, that one (the supreme person) is greater than all others. I will speak to you about the fundamentals of this one unique person. It is said that they are the only source of the many people, who, having gained **immaterial** *existence (nirguṇam), permanently shelter themselves within that great universal, also immaterial, first-person.*

"Listen, son, to how one explains this eternal, immutable, indestructible, immeasurable person who goes everywhere. They cannot be seen by you, by me or by anyone else. They are understood as universal, with and without attributes of matter, and can only be perceived through knowledge.

"They do not have a body, but reside in all bodies. Even though they reside in bodies, they are not tainted by actions. My inner higher self, and yours, and everyone's, combined with each respective body, is the observer who can never, in any way, be perceived. This unique person, as universal head, universal arm, universal foot, eye, or nostril, goes alone through their own fields, stopping when they find comfort. The fields, certainly, are bodies. The seeds are good and bad deeds. That higher self of yoga (the 'person') knows this, which is why they are called the 'knower of the field.'

"No creature is able to know the dynamics (gati) of their arrival or departure from this body. Only with the guidance of Sāṁkhya and yoga do we know what these steps are like. I have thought about the dynamic of this (person), but I do not know (yet) about their supreme dynamics (uttama). However, I will speak according to my knowledge of the eternal person, of their uniqueness and greatness, for they are known as a unique person, called the 'Great Person.'

"The fire, which is only one, is lit many times. The sun, which is only one, is the only source of burns. The wind, which is only one, blows many times in the world. The great ocean is the only source of water. And this

unique person without the attributes of matter, is invested in all forms, which are supported by this same person without attributes.

"Having abandoned everything that is produced by the attributes (guṇas) of matter; having abandoned all actions, good or bad; having abandoned both the truth and the lie; in this way (a creature) becomes one without the attributes of matter. Having also experienced that inconceivable fourfold subtle existence, one who knows how to act without arrogance can reach the resplendent person.

*"As such, some want (to see the person as) the supreme higher self (**Paramātmā**). Other scholars of the experience of knowledge (want to see the person as) the higher self, the only higher self. In this case, the one who is the supreme higher self is said to be eternally without the attributes of matter. They are known as Nārāyaṇa. This person is the higher self of all (beings). And is not tainted by the fruits (of actions), just as the lotus leaf is not affected by contact with the water.*

*"But that higher self connected to action (**Karmātmā**), who is another higher self, is aligned (to the supreme higher self) by the bonds of liberation. They are seventeen (combined natures) and are aligned (with the supreme higher self) by (numerical) factors. This is how the plural person was described to you, step-by-step.*

*"One who, as a whole, houses the fabric of the world, is the highest thing that can be known. They are that which can be perceived, (they are) the perceiver, the thinker, the thinkable, the devourer, that which can be devoured, that which senses smell, the smells, that which touches, the palpable, that which sees, the visible, that which hears, the audible, the knower, that which can be known, with or without attributes (simultaneously). They are called **Pradhānam** and have the attributes of matter in balance. They are eternal, permanent, and unchanging.*

*"That which is the original ordination of the creator in the form of a creature (Dhātā[9]), the sages (viprās) call **Aniruddham** ('uncontained'). In the world, they are like a Vedic ritual. A very fitting prayer. Only that which may come into being pertains to them. Gods and munis peacefully offer them their portions in sacrifice, by the fire of the East.*

"I, Brahmā, the first lord of the creatures, was created by them (the

---

[9] Dhātā corresponds here to the Vedic ordaining god Savitā.

Universal Person) and you were created by me. From me came the changeable and fixed universe, and all the Vedas with their secrets, o my son. That person, split into four, can play as they wish. Therefore, only that person themselves is really Bhagavān, awakened from one's own experience.

"This I have told you, my son, is the perfect answer to your question. This is also explained with the same clarity in the Sāṁkhya doctrine and in yoga."

This passage from the Mahābhāratam was written with vocabulary that simulates the older Vedic cultural environment, which seems to indicate that the content is very old. The Vedic context is used in this text because it is part of an extensive debate that took place in the past about the true meaning of the Hymn to Puruṣa[10] ('Hymn to the Person,' one of the compositions found in the Ṛg Veda), one of the most important Vedic chants. The debate, which lasted millennia, sought to clarify who this universal person was who was sacrificed by the gods in order to reach heaven and immortality.

This debate about the nature of this person is the context in which the concept of meditation developed. The two philosophical doctrines from which we extract the essence of meditation - Sāṁkhya and Yoga - originated from the search for answers to these questions about the interpretation of the Hymn to Puruṣa. For this very reason, these two doctrines are considered an integral part of Brahminism (the religious and social system of orthodox Hinduism), which has its cultural foundations in the Vedas.

The two chapters of the Mahābhāratam we partially reproduced above will help us to reflect on personhood in meditation. But for this to be possible, we must first understand what this 'person' is that the word 'Puruṣa' refers to. What does it mean to be a 'person' in this case? We can begin to answer this by understanding this 'person' as a structural component of speech. A bit of grammar will help us to better understand this 'person' inside and outside of speech.

The grammatical person is a representation of the position assumed by a participant within the context of speech. Within a grammatical structure, there are three possible positions a 'person' can assume: one who

---

[10] Ṛg Veda, hymn 10.90

produces speech (first-person); one to whom speech is addressed (second-person); one who is only referred to as an object in speech (third-person). The grammatical person exists at the point where the phenomenon of language connects to that of consciousness. Speech, by default, is consciously produced and holds intentional meaning that manifests the inner strength of the person who is speaking.

The ability to express oneself in such a way that the manifestation of this inner strength can be perceived and understood in some way by another closes this circuit of personhood. The person that we are looking for is revealed by the subjective intention to be expressed and by the initiative of constructing speech with that purpose - whatever the language that is used for this. Grammar shows us that the first-person is the point-of-view that corresponds perfectly with this model, given that the second-person is only the recipient and the third-person is itself the object of speech.

For us to ensure that we are on the right path to find the 'person' in meditation, in accordance with the doctrines of Sāṁkhya and Yoga, we need to check what Sanskrit grammar says about points-of-view, or 'persons' in the structure of the language. To begin with, Sanskrit has the same structure of three points-of-view, or 'persons' and all three are called 'Puruṣa.' The positions of each person, or points-of-view, in speech are also the same, although they are presented in the reverse order to the one we use. The table below illustrates the similarities and differences between the Sanskrit standard and ours:

Sanskrit	Translation	Our standard
Prathamapuruṣa	*First-person*	Third-person
Madhyamapuruṣa	*Middle person*	Second-person
Uttamapuruṣa	*Supreme person*	First-person

Table 1: Table comparing points-of-view or 'persons' according to our standard and the Sanskrit standard

One can speculate that the order in which the points-of-view or 'persons' are described in Sanskrit indicate a solid comprehension of the genesis of the 'self' in human consciousness. In the first phase (which is equivalent to our third-person), the newborn's perception of self is built through the body, which merges with other objects in the environment. In the next phase (middle person), the acquisition of speech allows the child to perceive themself as a person, through others. Self-awareness begins in the third phase, in which the real person (no longer mirrored in the 'other') emerges as a force that causes the mind to become a tool with which to communicate with the world.

It is important to note the great importance given to the first-person, which in Sanskrit is given the name of the power of creation of the universe, Uttama Puruṣa (or Puruṣottama, the 'supreme person'). It is the only path that leads to the essential person, the higher self within each individual, while the other two points-of-view, or 'persons' are only indications that point indirectly in the direction that should be followed.

The inflection used in 'impersonal' verbs, that in Sanskrit are called 'bhāvakartṛkā' (verbs 'which make their own state the subject of the action'), reinforces the strong relationship between the first-person perspective in speech and personhood. Impersonal verbs are characterized by the absence of a point-of-view or 'person' that can assume agency for the event that is being referred to. Usually, they are verbs that allude to actions that take place in nature, without a subject, such as 'to rain.' The necessity to inflect the verb in an impersonal way makes it so that the third-person format - the least personal of the three - is always chosen in these cases, and never the second- or first-person formats.

In any case, the simple fact that our first-person is called by the same word that identifies the Creator of the Universe is already quite eloquent. It is testament to the fact that the doctrines of Sāṁkhya and Yoga, which derive their reflections from the Hymn to Puruṣa, base their discussions on the dimension of the first-person experience.

Let us return now to the brief dialogue between Brahmā and his son Rudra, to see if it is possible to extract from that section any other guidance regarding the nature of the person sought by meditation.

4. The Fourfold Nature of the Person

In the previous chapter, we presented a translated section of the Sanskrit epic Mahābhāratam, which is a part of the discussion about the Hymn
to Puruṣa. In it, Brahmā says twice that the *cosmic person* (Puruṣa) is fourfold. The first time, he says *"Having also experienced that inconceivable
fourfold subtle existence, one who knows how to act without arrogance can
reach the resplendent person."* This phrase promises enlightenment for the
meditator who has experienced a fourfold subtle existence that can not be
reached through reason - that is, one that is inconceivable to the non-med-
itative mind. In the second reference, Brahmā says: *"The person, split into
four, can play as they wish."* A clear indication that this fourfold 'person' is
in command when they manifest. If we understand these two comments
made by Brahmā as generic references to the human condition, this fourfold 'person' is the self that lives within each of us. What Brahmā says, to
simplify it a bit, is that each creature is actually a combination of four people in one. This concept of the quadruplicity of the person is found in the
Vedic hymn dedicated to Puruṣa, which says:

> *"One quarter of this (person) are the creatures, the world. Three quar-
> ters are immortality in the Heavens. The person (Puruṣa) went up with
> the top three quarters, (but) their (remaining) quarter was here once
> again."* [11]

Three parts of the person move up, but, a fourth part holds them down
here, like an anchor. It is very clear in this verse that the four parts are part
of the same one person. The Mahābhāratam narrative refers to each of the
four components with different names: Paramātmā, Karmātmā,

---

[11] Ṛg Veda 10.90.3-4

Pradhānam and Aniruddham. A brief description of each can be found in that text. But it may be interesting to examine each of the four components again, with a bit more attention. Paramātmā and Karmātmā are distinguished by numerical opposition, as the first is singular and the second is plural. If we use the first-person pronoun for both of them, one is the supreme, unique 'self' while the other is the 'self' of the body (since the body is a multiplicity organized to live as one person). Paramātmā and Pradhānam are both eternal and immutable but the second is linked to attributes of matter, although these attributes are 'in balance.' Pradhānam, therefore, is the spiritual 'self' capable of manifesting in matter - in the form of Dharma. Finally, Aniruddham (literally the 'un-recoiled') seems to represent the 'self' of the mind, which, according to the Yoga doctrine, needs to reach the condition of 'recoiled' (*niruddham*) for the person to manifest fully.

If this interpretation is correct, we can conclude that the verses of the Hymn to Puruṣa offer indications about the inner dynamics of the person who meditates. These lines state that the person may ascend with the three higher fourths (Paramātmā, Aniruddham and Pradhānam), but returns to manifest again in the last fourth - Karmātmā. Is this a reference in the Ṛg Veda to the cycle of rebirth? Maybe. But there is no doubt that the mind, represented in the Mahābhāratam by Aniruddham, is portrayed as an unstable source of the problems faced by the fourfold person (Puruṣa), which ultimately makes the person return to the body (Karmātmā).

There are other references in the Ṛg Veda to the division of the person into four components. At least two other verses offer the possibility of helping us to understand this fourfold nature of the person. By examining these verses, it may be possible to better understand the problem that one seeks to solve through the process of meditation. One of the verses appears in a hymn describing the marriage between Sūryā Sāvitrī, daughter of the nocturnal Sun (Savitā), and the god Soma. The narrator of this hymn, whose authorship is attributed to Sūryā herself, speaks to the bride as follows:

"Soma found her first. Gandharva found her next. Her third lord was Agni. And her fourth (lord) was born of human beings." [12]

A wife with four husbands is a figurative way of describing a person with four individuals (four selves) within one, all of them wanting to take

---

[12] Ṛg Veda 10.85.40

control of their life. Many Hindu scholars believe that this verse means only that the gods Soma (the spirit present in herbs that produce spiritual elevation), Gandharva (guardian of Soma, which has great affinity with primordial matter), and Agni (fire), have the right to engage sexually any woman who reaches marriageable age. However, understanding that the verse is directed to Sūryā, the bride of the god Soma, it does not make sense to say that her current bridegroom, the fourth on the list, is 'born from humans.' Nor does it make sense for Soma, who is the bridegroom, to also appear at the top of the list. But the list begins to make sense when paired with the four Puruṣas found in the Mahābhāratam and the Hymn to Puruṣa.

Soma and Gandharva can be understood to align with Paramātmā and Pradhānam, while Agni aligns with the unrestrained Aniruddha and the one 'born of humans' (the human body) aligns with Karmātmā. In the verse of the Hymn to Puruṣa, Soma, Gandharva and Agni are the three quarters of the person that go toward heaven when they are forced to join with the one that was 'born of humans' that appears again in the material world. Compared in this way, the three models all seem to converge in a coherent way in the conception of a fourfold view of the 'self' that lives within each creature.

But there is still another Vedic verse that appears to shed more light on the information presented so far. It says:

"Language (vāc) is measured in four parts. The intelligent brahmins knew them. Three of them do not separate, hidden in a secret place (guhā). Humans speak the fourth part of language." [13]

This verse speaks about language, which is precisely the most important tool that a person has to express themselves. The separation of language in four parts suggests that the author of the verse has considered different tools of expression for each of the four persons referred to in the previous sections. But the author states that only one of the parts of language is actually spoken, while the other three are hidden together in a secret place.

This 'secret place' where three fourths of the language are hidden is traditionally located in the heart. It is as if it were a magical space suitable for sheltering and protecting the subtle riches so that they are not lost in

---

[13] Ṛg Veda 1.164.45

the gross world. Three parts of language, therefore, can be classified as 'subtle' or subjective, in contrast to the spoken or written word, which can be classified as the 'gross' or objective part of language that humans use to communicate with one another. This gross part of language certainly includes mental representations of objects that correspond with the conventional meanings of words, through which impersonal speech is constructed.

The subtle aspects of language can be called collectively by the term 'signification' ('artha' in Sanskrit). Signification includes resources such as context, figuration, and intention, which add meaning and depth to a discussion. Signification surpasses the limits of expression of the words themselves and offers language the capacity to express subtleties that would never be reached with only the formal meanings of words. It is precisely this subtle aspect of language that gives personhood to language and voice to Puruṣa. The person needs to express themselves in some way so that their existence can be recognized and their contribution to the order of the world be complete. This expression is only possible when the four instances of the person find an adequate way to present themselves to the world, giving an appropriate signification to their speech. So we can say, using a Sanskrit play on words, that the *goal* ('artha') of Puruṣa is simply to provide objects with *signification* ('artha' as well).

There is another Vedic composition, the Māṇḍūkya Upaniṣad, which reflects on the fourfold nature of the self. The excerpt of this upaniṣad pertinent to this topic is reproduced below:

"All of this is Brahma. This higher self is Brahma. This higher self is fourfold.

*"The first quarter is **Vaiśvānara**, he who enjoys gross existence, with nineteen faces and seven limbs, with awareness turned outward, in a state of wakefulness (awakened).*

*"The second quarter is **Taijasa**, he who enjoys the delicate, with nineteen faces and seven limbs, with awareness turned inward, in a dream state.*

*"That (state) in which no desire is desired, and no dream is seen, that is deep sleep (suṣuptam). The third quarter is **Prājña**, whose face is the heart (cetas - the consciousness of the heart), simply full of awareness (prajñāna), made of happiness (ānanda), he who enjoys happiness, made one with the state of deep sleep.*

"This is the lord (Īshvara) of all, who knows everything, this is the inner controller, this is the womb (yoni - the place of gestation) of everything, it is in fact the cause of existence and dissolution of creatures.

*"Neither with perception turned inward, nor with perception turned outward, nor with perception turned inward and outward simultaneously, neither filled with perceptivity, nor perceptive nor non-perceptive. It is not seen, one does not negotiate with it, one can not catch it, it does not have distinctive signs, one can not think of it, one can not point it out. It is the essence of the experience of a single 'self', it is the extinction of the multiplicity, it is calm, benign, non-dual, so it is thought to be **Caturtha** (a quarter). It is the higher self. It should be known."* [14]

The upaniṣad from which these phrases were taken derives its reflections from the verse in the Hymn to Puruṣa which discusses the quadruplicity of the person. Here, brahma (as a neutral concept distinct from the god Brahmā in the Mahābhāratam) is the quadruplicity found in one's self. As Vaiśvānara, he is the higher self in the physical body. Taijasa is the higher self in the mind. Prājña is the higher self in the heart. And Īśvara or Caturtha is the higher self without a precise location, but that can be found in the heart when the three previous selves are in harmony with one's personal dharma.

In this selected excerpt, the upaniṣad describes the multiplicity of a person, of which three parts combine to reveal a fourth part, which could command the combination of the other three. Although there are small differences between the cited sources, none of them contest the quadruplicity of Puruṣa. And the search for the integration of these four persons is part of the meditation process.

In the next chapter we will examine the way in which the Sāṁkhya doctrine treats this question of the multiplicity of personhood to construct its theory of the mind.

---

[14] Māṇḍūkya Upaniṣad 2 to 7

5. Personhood in Sāṁkhya

The Sāṁkhya doctrine is one of the oldest texts of contemplation produced in India. Fragmented references to this text are found in the oldest upaniṣads, whose composition date back more than a millennium prior to this current era. The original formulator of this doctrine was called Kapila and the oldest reference to him (relating him to Sāṁkhya) appears in the Śvetāśvatara Upaniṣad[15], a text credited to the very lineage of the followers of Sāṁkhya. There are many questions regarding the dates and historicity of the teachers of this doctrine, but there are some authoritative compositions about which we have more accurate information. The oldest of these compositions is called Sāṁkhya Kārikā (written by Īśvara Kṛṣṇa). We have copied some verses from this text here that will be used to illustrate the topic discussed in this chapter. We should explain that the Sāṁkhya described by this kārikā is a bit different than the Sāṁkhya described in the Mahābhāratam and in other sources, but these differences do not create any issues for the analysis we are doing here.

Sāṁkhya bases its logic on the personhood of the universe. It is the person (Puruṣa) who is at the beginning of the process that brings the universe into existence. It is from this original person that the tools for perceptive intelligence are derived. It can be said that, at the very beginning of the universe, there is already a cosmic person capable of perceiving, but there is not even a single object that can be perceived. The desire to perceive is the source of creation, as it brings into being the means of perception, which in turn creates matter for the formal, objective manifestation of life.

---

[15] Śvetāśvatara Upaniṣad 5.2

The person is, according to Sāmkhya, the starting point of the creation process. They are also the metaphysical base on which the subjective and objective worlds rest. The creation of the universe, according to Sāmkhya, follows an inverse path to the one conceived by scientific thought that still prevails today. For the scientist, the origin of the universe is found in the dynamics of the natural laws inherent to matter. Given proper initial conditions, these laws promote the emergence of progressively more complex organizations of matter - organic life - which, growing in complexity and integration, create conditions for the emergence of consciousness and personhood.

The two opposing versions are summarized on the table below:

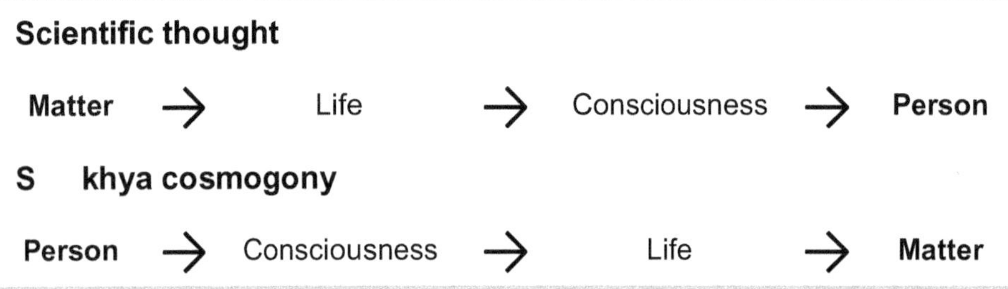

Table 2: Science versus Sāmkhya

Of course, even with all this simplification, the two systems are based on two very distinct methodological perspectives, which makes comparing them difficult. Therefore, we are going to focus only on the Sāmkhya version, so that we may understand the reasons that lead this doctrine to search for answers through a path that is so different from that of modern science, though no less correct.

The intrinsic difficulties in the model offered by Sāmkhya are of considerable magnitude, starting with the very definition of what (or who) Puruṣa is, the person to whom the origin of the world is attributed.

Sāmkhya Kārikā says, in its third verse:

"Primordial nature (Mūlaprakṛti) is not a derivative. Mahat and others are the seven derivatives of nature (Prakṛti). Sixteen are derivations (of the seven derivatives). The person (Puruṣa) is neither primordial nature, nor derived."

And, in verse 22:

"From Prakṛti arises Mahat, from which arises Ahaṁkāra and from this arises the group of sixteen. Through five of these sixteen arise the five elements."

In an elegant way, Īśvara Kṛṣṇa presented the 23 components of the structure of the universe from the point of view of the Sāṁkhya doctrine: Mahat (or buddhi); Ahaṁkāra; the five measurements that delimit the universe (Tanmātrāṇi); the mind (manas); the five organs of perception (Buddhīndriyāṇi); the five organs of action (Karmendriyāṇi); and the great elements (Mahābhūtāni). In describing the paths of derivation, he chose to focus on the groups, and in this way, avoid the challenge of relating each of the five great elements to each of the action organs and each of the corresponding organs of perception. He states that the five elements are derived from the five measurements of the universe (Tanmātrāṇi) without providing any further details. The ten organs and Manas (the 11th organ) are derived together from Ahaṁkāra.

The table below summarizes the content of these two verses according to Gauḍapāda's explanatory comments that accompany them. Each of the twenty-three components derived from primordial nature are called 'tattvam' and correspond to one functional principle found in the structure of every natural being. Note that only the seven derived components found in the upper half of the table produce their own derivations (indicated by arrows). The other sixteen, the mind being one of them, do not produce derivatives.

Puruṣa does not appear on this table because, according to verse 3, they are not part of primordial nature nor are derived from something else. Puruṣa is outside of the two sides of the process that gave rise to the universe. Puruṣa is not substance from which matter will be produced, nor the matter produced by this substance. But this does not remove Puruṣa from the story, as Puruṣa is explicitly referred to as the origin of everything in the universe. The Ṛg Veda, for example, confirms Puruṣa's leading role in the theater of the universe:

"Puruṣa is simply this entire universe, that which has already existed and that which will exist."[16]

Let us remember that Puruṣa represents personhood in meditation. But the concept of a cosmic Puruṣa seems to go beyond the realm of

---

[16] Ṛg Veda 10.90.2 – Puruṣa Sukta

meditation. We need to gather more textual information about Puruṣa's relationship to nature in order to clarify this further. Sāṃkhya Kārikā presents some more information that can serve us in this task.

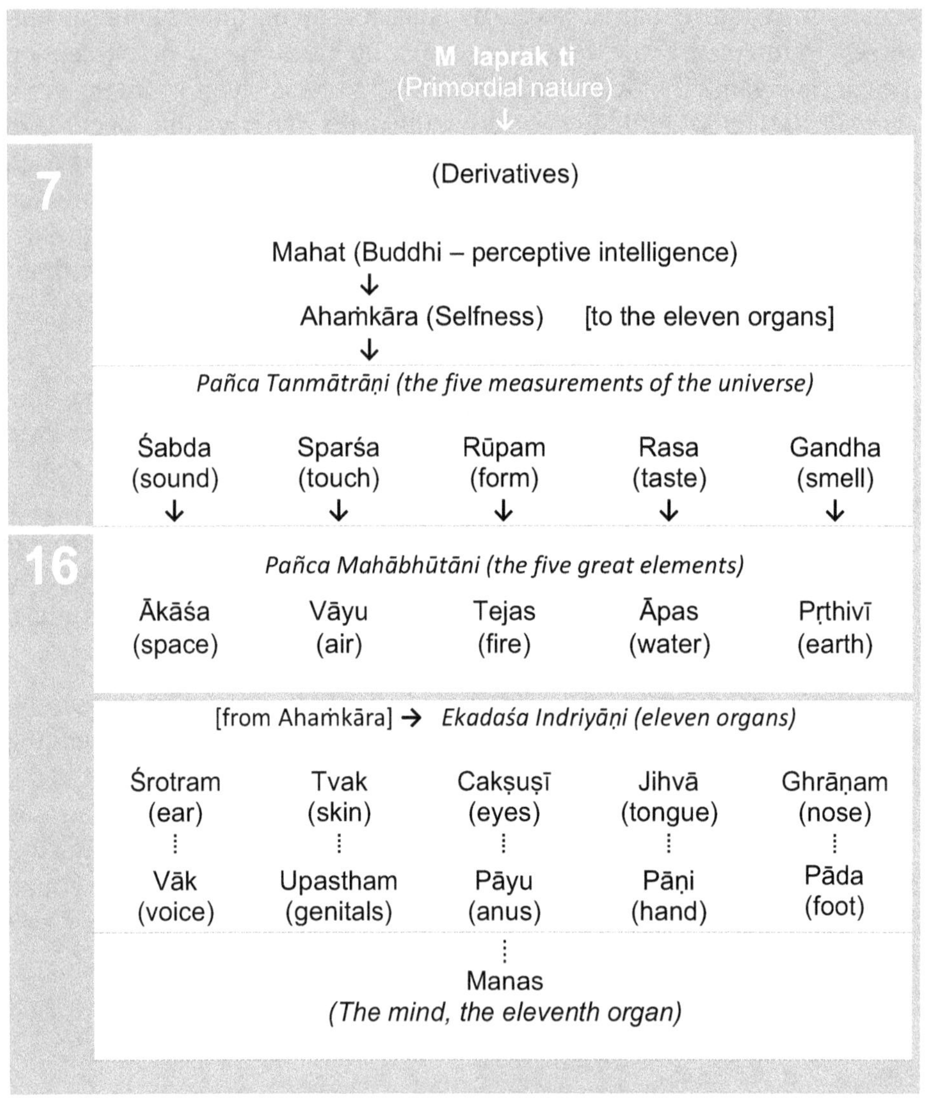

Table 3: Structure of nature

"Having the threefold quality (of nature), devoid of discernment, object of perception, generic, devoid of understanding, productive, this is the universal substance (Pradhānam) manifested. The opposite of this is Puruṣa." [17]

Gauḍapāda feels the need to clarify this definition of Puruṣa, obtained by opposition of the attributes of Pradhānam, and comments on this verse as follows:

"Manifested and unmanifested matter have the threefold quality (triguṇam). Puruṣa is devoid of these qualities.

"Manifested and unmanifested matter are devoid of discernment. Puruṣa is capable of discernment.

"So also are manifested and unmanifested matter objects of perception. Puruṣa is not an object of perception.

"So also are manifested and unmanifested matter generic (sāmānya). Puruṣa is individual.

"Manifested and unmanifested matter are devoid of understanding. Puruṣa has understanding.

"Manifested matter and Pradhānam are productive. Puruṣa is not productive. Nothing is produced from Puruṣa. That is why we say the 'opposite of this is Puruṣa.'" [18]

Gauḍapāda's commentary highlights the fact that "*nothing is produced from Puruṣa*" and is therefore the inverse of material nature, both manifested and unmanifested. But, at the same time, Puruṣa is recognized as a source of some actions that occur within the material scenario, such as the act of discerning or understanding. The Sāṃkhya doctrine, therefore, claims that some sort of relationship between Puruṣa and manifested nature is possible, one that transfers non-material characteristics to objects composed of matter. And this happens without Puruṣa losing the characteristic of immateriality.

Described in this way, it may seem that Puruṣa (the person within each creature) does not actually exist, since they are outside of universal nature. The comment also states that it is not possible to perceive Puruṣa as they

---

[17] Sāṃkhya Kārikā 11
[18] Sāṃkhya Kārikā Bhāṣya 11

are not an object of perception. But Sāṁkhya Kārikā strives to clarify that Puruṣa exists, even if not as an object, and gives some reasons for believing this:

"Because material bodies receive meaning from others; because (of the existence) of the inverse of the threefold quality (of matter), etc.; because of the establishment of command (over the body); because of the existence of the enjoyer; because of the existence of the activity that expresses isolation (of the enjoyer in relation to that which is enjoyed by the body); (it follows naturally that) Puruṣa exists." [19]

Note that the reasons listed by the author to demonstrate the existence of Puruṣa are built from logical needs, given the general conditions in which material nature is found. This verse is important to understand the dynamic that takes place between Puruṣa and nature.

The first logical need felt by the philosopher Īśvara Kṛṣṇa (the author of the Kārikā) arises from the belief that material bodies are produced by nature without their own signification, and that they need to receive this signification from others. Here we can understand 'others' as a reference to other bodies in nature, but these are also created without their own signification, which is why we must acknowledge their inability to give to the other what they themselves do not possess. Discarding this alternative, the term 'others' can also be understood as a reference to a subjective category of entities, outside of the domain of objective nature. Immaterial entities, such as, for example, the meaning of words - ideas that represent material objects which words identify. Or even more immaterial entities, such as the force of signification itself, which creates and maintains the links between words and their meanings. The bridge that allows for the exchange between Puruṣa and material nature may certainly be signification (artha), an abundant force in language, that occupies an axial position: language is only possible when the phenomenon of signification is present.

But the Sāṁkhya doctrine still needs to explain how Puruṣa can interfere with the phenomenon of nature without being a part of nature itself. Any force that acts on any system of matter must necessarily be a part of that system. Verse 17, cited above, speaks to the need for establishing command over the body, a command that Īśvara Kṛṣṇa attributes to Puruṣa, who, however, is outside of the material universe.

---

[19] Sāṁkhya Kārikā 17

Gauḍapāda's commentary on verse 17 adds some clarifying information about what followers of Sāṁkhya thought about the nature of Puruṣa, considering it to be at the same time distinct from the fabric of matter and in some way integrated and linked to it:

(...)

"Why (is it said) that Puruṣa exists? Because material bodies receive their meaning from another (being). This (body) made up of mahat and other (components) receives its meaning from Puruṣa. Let us suppose (this body) is devoid of meaning, like a paryaṅka. Just as each paryaṅka is a combination of a sash to keep the legs slightly lifted (like a flower), a footrest, a cotton blanket and a cloth seat, (a combination) that makes sense for someone else, but not for oneself. Of the components of paryaṅka, like the lifting of the legs and so on, none should be made for (give mutual signification to) any other. Hence it follows that there is a person (Puruṣa) who rests on the paryaṅka, from whom the paryaṅka derives its meaning [the paryaṅka does not extract its meaning from any of its components, but only from the person who makes use of it]. This (human) body composed of the five great elements takes on meaning from another (being). Puruṣa exists, to whom this body capable of being enjoyed belongs, produced in an enjoyable form composed of mahat and other components.

(...)

"[Regarding command]: Just as a chariot harnessed to horses, capable of jumping, trotting or running, moves at the command of a coachman, so the body (moves) at the command of the higher self (ātmā). So, it is also said in Ṣaṣṭitantra:[20] *'Pradhānam moves under command of Puruṣa'."* [21]

In the first line of the above quote, confirming the existence of Puruṣa, Gauḍapāda clarifies that, although the material body is composed of principles such as mahat (perceptive intelligence), ahaṁkāra (selfness), manas (relational mind) and others, this body is 'acetanam,' that is, lacking of understanding or consciousness. He rules out any possibility of a human body being endowed with understanding, as it is a material object like any other, endowed only with the properties of material nature. The capacity for

---

[20] Writing of the sage Pañcaśikha, known only from citations.
[21] Sāṁkhya Kārikā Bhāṣya 17

understanding is a characteristic unique to the person (Puruṣa) that uses the body.

He also clarifies that the signification is not an intrinsic property of the object but is an attribute that the object receives from the person who is using it. Gauḍapāda gives the example of paryaṅkāsanam, a set of artifacts created for the comfort of the meditator, which have no signification except for the person who uses them. It is the enjoyer, Puruṣa, who gives signification to any object.

The second line of the quote uses the image of a carriage to illustrate the issue of the immaterial person's command of the actions of matter. The command of the coachman is key to understanding how intention ('saṁkalpa') of the person, who does not share the attributes of materiality, can affect the body and trigger mechanisms of a purely material nature. In order to drive the carriage, the coachman gives the horses signs of his intention, with shouts, noises or movements of the reigns. A language made up of very simple signs is sufficient to command the actions of the horses and guide the carriage along the desired path.

The human body, like the carriage, is moved by commands of the higher self (ātmā) or, on a larger scale, the universal substance (Pradhānam) moves driven by Puruṣa. The carriage attached to the horses, but without the command of the coachman, would park or drive aimlessly - its trajectory would turn into movement without any signification. The coachman, on the other hand, needs the carriage to travel through the material realm. There is mutual dependence here, which explains the reason for the union between the immaterial person and material nature.

In order to understand how Sāṁkhya resolves Puruṣa's interference with matter, one must carefully examine the explanation offered by Kārikā. The figure of the coachman who uses simple signals to command the horses brings us to an important question: if understanding is an attribute of Puruṣa, how can the horses understand the commands of the coachman? We can only answer this question if we accept, by the logic of Sāṁkhya, that Puruṣa is also present in the horses, giving them the ability to attribute signification to the signs of the driver, thus allowing them the ability to understand. We need to accept that Puruṣa (the person) who is expressed as a horse does indeed understand the language of the other Puruṣa who is expressed as the coachman. Language is the link that connects these two instances of Puruṣa, crossing the realm of material nature on its way. Command is made possible because the two persons (the horse and the coachman) understand and agree on the signification of the signs in the language being used. *Without **signification**, an exclusive attribute of Puruṣa, there is no command.*

The first-person perspective (to which signification and understanding are linked) characterizes the realm of the forces of Puruṣa, and the third-person perspective characterizes the realm of material forces. The two meet and integrate perfectly in the space of language. The body/spirit dichotomy, in the case of the meditator, is resolved in the same way as the 'acoustic body/meaning' dichotomy is resolved, in the case of the word[22]. The linguist Ferdinand de Saussure called these two indispensable psychological elements of the word 'signifier' and 'signified.' Sāṁkhya adds to this the idea that the 'body' (whether of a word, or of a human individual) carries with it the tool of isolation (*'kaivalyam'*) allowing it to detach itself from the rest of nature, transforming its generic characteristics into personal traits - which 'isolate' it from the rest. The person 'signified' by the body, on the other hand, carries the tool of 'vision' (darśanam, meaning 'the capacity to perceive') which allows the body the ability to understand. This topic is explored as follows in the Sāṁkhya Kārikā:

> *"Because of this union, the 'signifier' ('liṅgam', that is, Pradhānam), which is devoid of understanding, appears to be endowed with understanding. And in the same way, one who is indifferent (to action: Puruṣa) becomes similar to an agent, because of the agency of the attributes (guṇas) of matter.*
>
> *"Puruṣa has the tool (artha) of perception, just as Pradhānam has the tool of isolation (kaivalyam). When both are united, such as when a crippled person (Puruṣa) is united with the blind (Pradhānam), the creation (of the universe) (occurs)."* [23]

In the realm of signification, therefore, mutually dependent bonds are created between the materiality of the body and the immateriality of the person. We are born with the same dichotomy identified by linguists in words, precisely the characteristic that gives us the power to live and recreate life. This same power of the word is the one through which the universe is created. Sāṁkhya Kārikā helped us to find (in signification) the

---

[22] Ferdinand de Saussure. Cours de Linguistique Générale [annoté] (French Edition). Philaubooks. Part 1, Chapter 1.

[23] Sāṁkhya Kārikā 20 and 21

connection that gives Puruṣa access to the objective world. It is still necessary to clarify the process by which, using signification, Puruṣa manages to affect the course of the phenomena of material nature. It is precisely within this subjective field of signification, so familiar to poets and so rejected by scientists, that the process of meditation takes place. It is also there that the human spirit breaks free.

Gauḍapāda taught us in this chapter that Puruṣa is the source of understanding, discernment, and individuality. The manifested world is generic and shared, but the experience of meditation is personal and not shared. This suggests a way to add more clarity to our theoretical model of the process of meditation. A path into individuality.

6. Sustainability

Meditation is a practice through which the meditator is able to nullify multiplicity of character found within oneself by becoming identical only to one's own self. For one's mental state to stabilize and arrive at a point of sustainability, one must rely on Puruṣa as the only reference for personal identity. A sustainable life, from the perspective of yoga, is one in which there is no need for external stimuli for the mind to build motivation and enthusiasm. The meditative mind finds its motivation from within, and, for that reason, its goals will always be within reach of its practical ingenuity.

Although the mind, when free, is always looking for new information and reevaluating its present goals, when the mind becomes meditative, its curiosity is overseen by intuition. The mind that meditates rejects the significations brought in by others, unless they are compatible with its own significations. This mental mechanism of rejecting that which is not aligned with one's personal characteristics aims to provide for sustainability and conviction in decision-making.

Whenever the mind is found affected by dualities, such as cold/hot, pleasure/pain, light/dark, success/failure, inside/outside, there is the urge to continually move between the two opposite extremes. If the mind gives in to this urge, it loses its desired state of balance. It may also lose part of its sensitivity for understanding things. From the perspective of the Sāṁkhya doctrine, loss of understanding corresponds to a weakening of the presence of Puruṣa in the mind, as is discussed in verses 20 and 21 of the Sāṁkhya Kārikā, presented in the previous chapter.

The continued practice of meditation increases how quickly the mind is able to return to its state of balance and understanding. The ability to remain in a comfortable balance between opposite concepts increases the cognitive acuity of the mind. Indifference to the natural tension that exists between opposing ideas can also be strengthened with meditation. The balanced mind of the meditator retains its responsiveness, even if strained. Because it has a clearer perception of the events around it, the meditator's mind is able to maintain a healthy indifference to the effects those events produce. Without being carried away by fear, pleasure, discomfort or any other immediate effect of these events, the meditative mind is better able to understand the true scope of what is happening and make more appropriate decisions regarding each event.

Not all dualities produce tensions harmful to the meditator's mental balance. Some dualities produce an integrating tension, such as that found in words, uniting signifier and signified. These are pairs that do not divide but integrate two distinct natures in one greater entity that surpasses its component parts. Integrated in their duality, words and other signs of communication are no longer just sounds or figures that represent objects, but become tools of personal expression, which is the foundation of any human relationship. They cease to be dual or plural and become singularities.

The signifier/signified duality, integrator of the word, is very similar to the duality that exists between Pradhānam and Puruṣa. Pradhānam, material nature, endowed with the capacity of isolation (kaivalyam), offers perception (of the mind) sensory stimuli grouped into individualized structures that are ready to receive signification from Puruṣa. The existence of a meaning for a material object is a sign of Puruṣa's own interference, who, in this way, inserts themselves in material nature, while still not being a part of it. In the case of a word, meaning is not a part of the sound or writing of the word, since the idea evoked by the word is of an immaterial and subjective nature. Therefore, although intertwined by the force of signification, the objective and subjective components of the word preserve their essential characteristics: what is objective continues to exist exclusively in the domain of objectivity; what is subjective remains in the domain of subjectivity. But these two domains, while preserving their independence, somehow touch each other, unite and gain, through words, the power, hitherto non-existent, to build a larger entity: signification.

The resulting word also surpasses its component parts in another sense, as a poetic image. The image is the soul of poetry, the most personal way of using the word, which gives it this power to overcome, capable of merging naturally even those components that would appear to be in conflict. The poetic image reconciles the irreconcilable, as it resolves in an integrative manner the semantic tensions between words, lending sustainability to the discourse.

In his essay called "The Image", the Mexican poet Octavio Paz says the following about this topic:

"(...) we use the word image to designate every verbal form, phrase, or group of phrases that the poet says and that together compose a poem. (...) Each image—or each poem made of images—contains many opposite or disparate meanings, which it embraces or reconciles without suppressing. Thus, Saint John speaks of 'silent music,' a phrase in which two apparently irreconcilable terms are allied. (...) Sleep and waking are bound together in Segismundo in an indissoluble, mysterious way. In Oedipus, liberty and destiny... The image is the key to the human condition." [24]

Thus, poetry, as a key that helps to decipher the human condition, can be seen as yet another tool available to the meditator. By reconciling opposing terms within discourse, poetry can reduce friction between dualities and help the meditator to find sustainable alignment where previously there was disruptive opposition. Poetry (*kāvyam*), in Sanskrit culture, has been recognized since Vedic times as the language of the sages - who are, thus, often called poets ('*kavi*'). All the authors of Vedic verses are called poets, both for the content and for the formal structure of their compositions.

Poetic words, charged with personality, are a perfect way of relating the first-person experience, as they are able to abandon the generic speech of the third-person, which can be said in another way, with other words. Octavio Paz explains this uniqueness of poetic discourse in the same text cited earlier:

"Every phrase has a reference to another, is susceptible to being explained by another. Thanks to the mobility of signs, words can be explained by words. (...) Every phrase means something that can be expressed or explained by another phrase. Consequently, the sense or meaning is a trying to say. Or rather: an utterance that can be said in another way. On the contrary, the meaning of the image is the image itself: it cannot be said with other words. The image explains itself.

---

[24] Paz, Octavio. The Bow and the Lyre (Texas Pan American Series). University of Texas Press. Kindle edition. (pos. 1363)

Nothing, except it, can say what it tries to say. Meaning and image are the same thing. A poem has no meaning other than its images." [25]

The personhood of the meditator, like the uniqueness of the poetic image, is resolved within itself, in the unique meeting of the *words* that it is composed of. The meditator becomes an individual only when they start to depend on only themselves, by choosing a life guided by their own opinions and values, respecting their own integrity.

Without this uniqueness and self-sufficiency, the person is not able to sustain themselves as an individual and becomes a generic character, a haunted sum of collective characteristics - inflected in the third-person. They are not a singular individual but a multiplicity, a plural individual whose subjectivity creates the imminent danger of disintegration. Each of their components is exclusive, meaning the other components must be annulled in order for each to manifest itself. In this scenario, the multiplicities would never unify.

Quoting Paz again in the same essay:

"(...) There are, in short, images that achieve what seems to be a logical as well as a linguistic impossibility: the marriage of opposites. In them all — scarcely visible or fully realized — is observed the same process: the plurality of the real is manifested or expressed as ultimate unity, while each element retains its essential singularity. Feathers are stones, without ceasing to be feathers. Language, turned in on itself, says that which by nature seemed to elude it. Poetic expression expresses the inexpressible." [26]

The construction of a poetic image is identical to the construction of a person's individuality. The poet's words express the unspeakable, while the individualized person expresses a *personal spirit*, a uniqueness, that cannot be translated into patterns shared by the community. Collective thinking is logical and standardized and, therefore, predictable and incapable of eliciting surprise. Individual expression is unique, original and surprising, full of enchantment and creative daring.

The deliberations of a collective person, or one who follows the herd

---

[25] Paz, Octavio. The Bow and the Lyre (Texas Pan American Series). University of Texas Press. Kindle edition. (pos. 1536)

[26] Idem. (pos. 1572)

(*paśuvat*, in Sanskrit) are based on the opinions of others; these deliberations come together in their mind in a diffuse way, constructing what we will call impersonal thought. In order to feel comfortable with their reliance on the collective, this individual's mind constructs an imagined conviction in which they are thinking and acting with autonomy and independence, despite actually being dependent on the opinion of others. To put it bluntly, their identity is false and cannot find solid ground that supports it.

The individual person of the meditator easily finds within themselves the foundation for a rich subjective life, which contrasts with the poverty of the life of the collective person, something we all experience to some extent. Through contact with the collective, the individual characteristics of the meditator stand out and become evident. This occurs naturally and causes an impact on the community, who, attracted by the differences they see in that individual person, feel obliged to relate to them in a different way. The process of meditation reveals the individual person, who is able to find support within themselves and who has the moral strength to express their own ideas - transforming their life into a poetic act.

Let's use this reflection to understand the nature of the spirit a bit better, from the point of view of Sanskrit culture. For this, we need to briefly review our conception of ethics, especially the concepts of 'good' and 'evil.' The 'collective' person needs simple and clear rules that clearly determine what can and cannot be done. Rules that draw a definitive line between 'good' and 'evil.' This is necessary to ensure a shared social coexistence, in which individual freedoms are adjusted to the values shared by the community. But the individual person, when involved in situations that require more difficult decisions to be made, may feel the need to break the rules that guide the collective, and which claim universality. Situations like this reveal a gap that sometimes exists between the collective beliefs and individual values held by that person.

This is what happens, for example, with Prince Arjuna of the Lunar Dynasty in the story described by the Bhagavad Gītā. He has the task of giving the order to start a war in which two armies will fight each other, but whose members, on both sides, belong to the same family. The need to follow the ethical rule of respect for family and the duty to protect it speaks more strongly to Arjuna's conscience, who hesitates and decides not to fight. He is afraid of making the wrong decision and causing great harm to his relatives and friends.

However, his cousin Kṛṣṇa speaks with him and, with arguments that mix reason and poetry, appeals to Arjuna's greater duty to support the Dharma (a set of values and principles that sustain a person or community) even if this seems to be a great evil. Kṛṣṇa uses first-person rhetoric and speaks as if he were the inner voice of Arjuna's heart in order to invoke more strength in his arguments. He says:

"Your dharma carried out poorly is better than the dharma of another well executed. It is better to die while following your own dharma. There is danger in the dharma of others. " [27]

What would the danger be in following someone else's dharma? There is certainly the danger of losing personal identity, which could lead to falsehood and from there, an even more destructive problem may arise: loss of sustainability. Although imitating a certain person is a behavior that, generally, can be easily identified - as is the case of the Elvis Presley impersonators that meet annually in Memphis, TN, for example - imitation of the collective is not always so easy to identify. Copying the behavior of the collective is a way of taking on a false originality, expressing an individuality that is not actually yours and, strictly speaking, does not belong to anyone. It only allows the person to make themselves into someone else, someone who can be considered an acceptable member of the group. But, since becoming someone else is impossible, while imitating a social standard may provide the comfort of being accepted by the collective, it will bring falsehood into one's life as well. And it reduces the capacity of the individual to contribute through their own personal characteristics to the evolution of the very rules and standards that regulate life in society.

Each member of a community should give body and voice to the psychological forces that are expressed through their authentic personal identity, for their own good and for the good of the collective. Strengthening this unique identity, which is manifested when expression is free and spontaneous, is the highest goal of the practice of meditation. When balance is achieved between personal and collective identity, the individual becomes a potential agent of social transformation. Only then can a sustainable relationship be consolidated between society and its members, that is, between the social order and the personal spirit of each person. This 'meditative' relationship of the individual with society is the inverse of the parasitic attitude adopted by a merely 'collective' person of the herd, one who

---

[27] Bhagavad Gītā, 3.35

only imitates social standards motivated by the desire to acquire some sort of personal benefit. When this parasitic attitude is abandoned, the individual's participation can benefit the community as well.

Returning to our discussion about ethics, it seems clear that the 'personal spirit,' referred to above, is beyond the concepts of good and evil. It is impossible to evaluate this personal spirit within the limits of the social perspective, as it is precisely this distinguishing force that can reformulate the rules of society. This spirit, which is connected to the first-person perspective, is what makes the individual be considered a better person, one who deserves to be imitated. In the Bhagavad Gītā, Kṛṣṇa says to Arjuna:

"Whatever the best one does [28], this is exactly what ordinary people will do. The world follows the standard set by this one." [29]

The higher self (ātmā or spirit) cannot be considered good or evil but must be carefully observed as the manifestation of this higher self is what gives signification to things (memories, scenes, objects, events, actions, etc.). Providing signification is the same as making something knowable. Knowledge only exists if it is accessible through memory, and memory is only capable of storing information when that information has some sort of signification. Information endowed with signification becomes knowledge. The ability to know is an attribute of the personhood of Puruṣa (Īśvara, the internal commander) and Patañjali, in the Yoga Sūtras, states that Īśvara hides *"the unsurpassed seed of all knowing"* [30]. Knowledge is only knowable because of Puruṣa, who gives it signification, but it is also Puruṣa that gives us the understanding to store, retrieve and use that knowledge. Although Puruṣa is not a part of the objective world, over time, they demonstrate how close they are to our daily life.

If there is no Puruṣa, a higher self, who can be classified as good or evil, or who fits into any kind of duality, the space in which these tensions manifest themselves will necessarily be restricted only to the mind. The mind is responsible for our perceptions (which can suffer distortions) and for the realization of our actions, whose meanings can be judged as good or evil, depending on the context in which they are manifested. The mind itself is responsible for judging our actions, which is subject to error.

---

[28] "the best one" in this verse is one whom others consider to be "the best."

[29] Bhagavad Gītā 3.21

[30] Yoga Sūtras 1.25

The act of killing a human being, for example, is certainly among the evilest actions, and should be avoided at any costs. But this perspective may change dramatically when, for example, the person who kills is a law enforcement agent and the person who dies is a psychopath who uses a child as a living shield to protect himself from a police siege. In the case of Arjuna, who is a warrior leader specialized in using the bow and arrow, killing his adversary is something that he is expected to know how to do effectively and without hesitation when the need arises. But Arjuna's mind is fixated on contextual details that confuse his understanding and challenge the sustainability of his personal convictions. The ethical question of good and evil is a dangerous matter for the mind, which, agitated, unstable and reactive, is always very close to treading the paths of error.

We saw in chapter 4 that Puruṣa can manifest themselves in four instances within each person. The term used in yoga literature for 'instance' is '*avasthiti.*' Of the four instances, three are associated and correlates of (objective or subjective) material nature: the body, the mind and the heart. The fourth instance manifests itself when the other three internally align with Puruṣa and integrate with each other, in the form of a unified structure, which allows for the expression of Paramātmā. The body and the heart align easily with Puruṣa, but the mind finds this task difficult. This is why the basic goal of meditation is to correct the workings of the mind.

The mind works with sensory stimuli brought in by the body and stitches them to meanings offered by the heart. We need to discover the origin of the disturbances of our mind. Therefore, we will devote the next chapter to taking a closer look at the nature of the mind and how it works.

7. The Internal Instrument

There are certain things that we are so familiar with that we rarely think about their nature or see any reason to doubt their existence. The mind is one of those things, so evidently real that it seems absurd to think that it could be, as some would have it, only an illusion created by the functioning of our neurons. Although it is mainly correlated with bodily functions, the mind seems to be part of another category of things, distinct from material nature. It just isn't clear what these sorts of things would be that define the category to which the mind belongs. Reflecting a bit more on the nature of the mind can be very useful for someone who wants to try meditation. The mind is the main instrument for meditation; but it carries an intrinsic instability, which can be considered the main obstacle that stands in the way of a meditator's success.

The nature of the mind, mental phenomena and actions have long fascinated and troubled thinkers around the world. In Sanskrit culture, there are many fascinated by this topic who provide very interesting responses to the question "*what is the mind?*". But, before proceeding down this path, it would be most prudent for us to consult some dictionary definitions to see what they have to say about the mind.

Dictionaries are not very substantive in their definitions of the mind. It is easy to find vague and evasive definitions such as "*the **element** or **complex of elements** in an individual that feels, perceives, thinks, deliberates, and, above all, reasons*", or "***source** of psychic and intellectual activity.*" One might note that these definitions do not elucidate the nature of this 'element' or this 'source' to which they refer.

Specialized literature, of scientific nature, describes the nature of the mind in an equally evasive way, choosing to explain it through the nature of other smaller entities. The Portuguese neuroscientist António Damásio says the following:

> *"Minds emerge when the activity of small circuits is organized across large networks so as to compose momentary patterns. The patterns represent things and events located outside the brain, either in the body or in the external world, but some patterns also represent the brain's own processing of other patterns."* [31]

Damásio speaks for many of his colleagues when he defines the mind as an emergent phenomenon, derived from the momentary complexities produced by the connections between neurons in the brain. If there were no formation of complex structures for the passage of electrical charges between thousands or millions of nerve cells in an interconnected network, the mind would not manifest itself. When the neural network forms, the mind emerges and hovers above the nervous system. Damásio adds:

> *"Our intuition tells us that the mercurial, fleeting business of the mind lacks physical extension. I believe this intuition is false and attributable to the limitations of the unaided self."* [32]

While alluring in its simplicity, this scientific model of the mind makes the existence of free will very unlikely. According to these postulations, all mental processes emerge as by-products of certain biological actions and are therefore unable to intentionally affect the biological functioning of the objective body. This model, which prevails in the academic world today, suggests that it would be possible to map the brain circuits that are active at the moment when a certain mental activity happens, which would establish a reciprocal relationship (or correlation) between the subjective mental activity and the objective activity of a certain group of neurons. This model is supported by the fact that study after study has confirmed the correlation between the brain and the mind, while a complex map of the neural circuits related to well-defined mental functions is being built with the help of new digital image technology.

There is, however, at least one mental activity for which there seems to be no correlate in the brain: the experience of the first-person. This lasting experience, which persists throughout life, and which gives us a

---

[31] Damasio, Antonio in "Self Comes to Mind." 2010. New York, Knopf Doubleday Publishing Group. Kindle edition. (pos. 362)
[32] Cited text. Pos. 312.

privileged seat for any other experience, is responsible for weaving the self to the body. The first-person experience gives the mind a very special depth that surpasses everything that scientific thought has been able to offer, until today, as an explanation for its nature.

Of course, there are people who 'solve' the problem through denial, attributing consciousness to an illusory existence. This is, for example, the opinion of Daniel Dennett, a philosopher and cognitive scientist (at Tufts University), who states, at the beginning of one of his books:

"In the chapters that follow, I will attempt to explain consciousness. More precisely, I will explain the various phenomena that compose what we call consciousness, showing how they are all physical effects of the brain's activities, how these activities evolved, and how they give rise to illusions about their own powers and properties." [33]

Dennett strives to explain that the mind, consciousness, and 'self' are just hallucinations of the brain that help humans in the process of biological evolution, to resist the temptation to eat one's own hand when hungry, for example. A proposition that is acceptable only for those who like this type of rhetoric. For the rest of us, there is still no scientific theory that satisfactorily explains the experience of the first-person. On this particular topic, science leaves us helpless.

We will return to the topic of consciousness later in chapter 9. For now, it is better for us to abandon modern thought and return to Sanskrit culture, which offers some paths for reflection that are very old, like those that were introduced when we discussed the personhood of Puruṣa. Let's see if this culture can teach us more about the first-person experience, this phenomenon that gives lived meaning to our perceptions and intentionality to our actions.

To arrive at the Sanskrit concept of the mind, we need to understand something about a mysterious power in which the mind somehow participates. Sanskrit tradition believes in the existence of a natural power capable of interfering with the signals that travel along the pathways of the nervous system, brought in by our organs of perception, introducing the concept of a 'self' into our system, a 'self' who 'enjoys', or lives, our experiences. This power is called *Cit* and is directly related to the higher self, or

---

[33] Dennett, Daniel C. "Consciousness Explained" 2017, New York, Little, Brown and Company, Kindle Edition. (pos. 404) – written in 1991

ātmā. Due to this powerful presence, the mind is opened to the first-person perspective. Sāyaṇa Mādhava Ācārya, a 14th century Indian scholar, in his analysis of the philosophical system proposed in the Yoga Sūtras of Patañjali, summarizes this force of Cit in a few words:

> *"The power of the enjoyer is the power of Cit, it is said. It is simply one's own higher self."* [34]

The power of Cit (*cicchakti*) or the power of Citi (*citiśakti*[35]), is the result and the testimony of the direct interference of Puruṣa, that is, of the self in material nature. It manifests itself as a trail of information that travels through the body, as *pratyakṣas* (sensory stimuli) or *vikalpas* (imaginary stimuli) in search of some form of meaning. It is Puruṣa who offers meaning (*puruṣārtha*) to this raw information, thus establishing the starting point for the construction of language. The action of Cit, as can be seen, is responsible for the organization of the subjective life of creatures, resulting in the formation of the mind (antaḥkaraṇam), its main instrument.

In this context, the mind can be defined as the subjective space within which Cit gives rise to the light of consciousness (*cetanam*). Activity that takes place in this subjective space of the mind is both material activity of Prakṛti and direct action of Puruṣa. This is the very nature of words, where the objective forms of the sounds of the spoken word or the graphic signs of the written word are combined with the subjective meanings of these words. Just as words do not exist without these two components made of such different natures, the mind also does not exist without the integration of the objective body and the subjective self.

From the power of Cit an explosion of meaning is born, a linguistic phenomenon called *sphoṭa* that allows us to understand what the words are saying. Sphoṭa connects the discourse of second-person or third-person speech to the first-person consciousness. This same explosion of meaning, when it occurs in the mind, reveals the unique personal characteristics that define an individual's identity and provide for intentionality in their actions. Cit's power also reveals evidence, permeating the intelligent fabric of words, of the presence of a self in the other, of a person in the interlocutor. This gives rise to the second-person, the 'you' who exists at the other end of communication.

---

[34] Sarva Darśana Saṁgraha 15,19-20
[35] This is the form used by Patañjali in the Yoga Sūtras 4.34.

The word *'cittam'* adopted by Patañjali to identify the mind is derived from the word 'Cit' - used as a verbal root to express the action of 'understanding,' 'being aware.' Many other Sanskrit words have been translated as meaning 'the mind', creating some confusion in understanding the process of meditation. However, in Sanskrit literature that discusses meditation, only the words *antaḥkaraṇam* (literally: 'internal instrument') and *cittam* can be considered equivalent to the word 'mind.' An older term '*manas*' is sometimes used as a synonym for cittam or antaḥkaraṇam, although it is more aptly defined as just one of the components of the mind, as we will see ahead. Patañjali uses only the word 'cittam' and does not ever refer to antaḥkaraṇam, nor does Vyāsa in his commentary on the Yoga Sūtras. It is possible that in Patañjali's time, the expression antaḥkaraṇam had not yet received the technical meaning that made it equivalent to cittam in the literature that discusses meditation.

In the literature of yoga, we see the mind called antaḥkaraṇam by Svātmarāma[36], in the mid-14th century. Before that, in the 11th century, Gorakṣanātha, in the Siddha Siddhānta Paddhati, described characteristics of antaḥkaraṇam, saying that it is made up of five components: buddhi, ahaṁkāra, manas, cittam and caitanyam[37]. Note that in this particular text, cittam was converted into simply a component of antaḥkaraṇam. In other texts, however, cittam is presented as a synonym for antaḥkaraṇam. In 1896, Swāmi Vivekānanda states his agreement with the partial overlap between antaḥkaraṇam and cittam when he says the following, in his commentary on the Yoga Sūtras:

"The organs (Indriyas), together with the mind (Manas), the determinative faculty (Buddhi), and egoism (Ahamkâra), form the group called the Antahkarana (the internal instrument). They are but various processes in the mind-stuff, called Chitta." [38]

Long before this, in the beginning of the 9th Century, Ādi Śaṁkarācārya already claimed that cittam is antaḥkaraṇam in his commentary on verse 4.21 of the Bhagavad Gītā. He suggests that the mind is the instrument through which the higher self can become manifest in the

---

36 Haṭha Yoga Pradīpikā, verses 2.28 and 4.99
37 Siddha Siddhānta Paddhati, in verses 1.43-48
38 "Complete Works of Swami Vivekananda", volume 1, "Raja Yoga", "Patanjali's Yoga Aphorisms", "Chapter I. Concentration: Its Spiritual Uses", commentary on sūtra 1.2 (pos. 2673)

material body as *bhūtātmā*:

> *"(...) as for the expression of 'cittātmā', 'cittam' is antaḥkaraṇam (the internal instrument) and 'ātmā' is the external (bodily) aggregate of the instruments of action (....)."* [39]

Īśvara Kṛṣṇa, in the 4th century, predates Śaṁkara in this idea of the mind as an internal instrument[40]. Gauḍapāda, in the beginning of the 8th century, explains that antaḥkaraṇam is composed of three principles: buddhi, ahaṁkāra and manas[41]. The Sāṁkhya Kārikā, in verse 30 (and respective commentary by Gauḍapāda), explains that antaḥkaraṇam works by integrating its three components with each of the organs of perception in order to process the fragmented information brought in by sensory organs to the subjective space of the mind. Each of the three components of the mind makes a specific contribution to the dynamics of mental activities:

a) Manas creates connections between the different fragments that bring in sensory information and relates them to other information that can be added to the thought-building process. It is probably manas that Patañjali is referring to when he uses the term '*bandhakaraṇam*' (binding agent) in sūtra 3.39. In fact, it is manas that should be credited for categorizing the ideas that inhabit the mind. It is this force that, within flexible limits, defines our preferences, our desires and our aversions, applying labels (not always correctly) to our experiences.

b) Ahaṁkāra's contribution essentially consists of adjusting the movement of information labeled by manas, so that this information can be directed to the self or so that it gravitates around this self, creating a sense of 'me' or 'mine.' With the help of ahaṁkāra, the mind is also able to appropriate other people's thoughts, making them seem to be their own.

c) Buddhi adds intelligence to thought, articulating it coherently and preparing it to receive and incorporate signification offered by Puruṣa (*puruṣārtha*). This signification expresses the unique personhood of each thinking individual.

These three components of antaḥkaraṇam added to the self lead us

---

[39] Bhagavad Gītā Bhāṣya 4.21
[40] Sāṁkhya Kārikā 33
[41] Sāṁkhya Kārikā Bhāṣya 33

once again to the quadruplicity of the thinking person. Only this time, it is seen through the structure of the components of the mind as an internal instrument, as described in the Sāṁkhya doctrine. But this is not the point that we are focusing on at this time.

The Yoga Sūtra Bhāṣya Vivaraṇam is another text that confirms the identity of cittam as antaḥkaraṇam. In the commentary of this text on sūtra 2.6, for example, the mind (*antaḥkaraṇam*) is referred to as an instrument (*upakaraṇam*) for Puruṣa. Vyāsa's commentary on this sūtra says:

"Puruṣa is the force of pure vision (dṛś) and buddhi is the force of vision of the experience (darśanam) (...)." [42]

The mind sees nothing, in reality, for it is not endowed with this capacity. It only processes and transports information collected through the sensory organs, or that it produces for itself using imagination. The mind is not the self but it is the only instrument that has the ability to bring the essence (*sattvam*) of perception to the self (*sākṣī*) so that it can see. Hence the importance of the mind for meditation: only the mind can ensure that perception is given over to Puruṣa, who is the only enjoyer (*bhoktā*) of the experience.

The mind should be permanently connected to Puruṣa, whom it serves, for it is the main conduit of the force of perception (*citiśakti*), responsible for bringing this force into the fabric of nature. Sanskrit literature regarding meditation states that the mind needs to manifest the *sattvam* quality in order to establish a functional connection with Puruṣa. If the predominant quality of the mind's activities is *tamas* or *rajas*, it loses its serenity and ends up manifesting conditions that limit its capacity to serve Puruṣa.

In the next chapter, a brief examination will be made of the conditions that challenge or even prevent the mind from fulfilling this main task. We will see how flaws in the system transform the mind into a source of problems, when it should be the source of all solutions.

---

[42] Yoga Sūtra Bhāṣya 2.6

8. System Flaws

The mind is a fantastic instrument with a wealth of resources for processing information. We take its functional availability for granted whenever we need to assess situations for decision making. We have confidence in the mind's capacity to organize the information it receives, identify dangers or challenges, and quickly find solutions for everything. The confidence we entrust to the mind makes life serene and comfortable, protected by a sense of predictability and security.

Behind this reliability of the mind, however, a hidden danger awaits the meditator. Among its many capabilities, there is one that can have very serious consequences, and can pose a threat to the physical integrity and the subjective balance of the mind itself. Its ability to perceive the possibilities of connection between objects in the external world can lead to a feeling of inadequacy or lack of belonging. Stuck between the immateriality of the self and the robust materiality of the objective body, the mind does not find a domain that adequately corresponds to it. The mind is not all material, though it is not immaterial either, because it does not even exist as an autonomous entity, independent of itself. The internal instrument, with all of its capabilities and weaknesses, only exists as a result of the integration of two apparently irreconcilable natures: material nature and immaterial nature. The mind depends on both to gain an existence that reveals itself as both real and illusory.

This is perhaps the biggest flaw of our internal information processing system. Unable to identify with material nature and, at the same time, unable to identify with immaterial nature, the mind swings like a pendulum, at times moving toward the passive and inert behavior of matter (*'tamas'* quality) and at times moving toward the subtle immutability of the immaterial entities ('*sattvam*' quality). Overtaken by the predominance of the '*rajas*' quality of nature, the mind maintains an unstable balance, moving constantly between those two poles (tamas and sattvam). Life ends up being uncomfortable, characterized by the oppression of these polarities, which makes the mind *desire* silence, integration and settling (*prasādanam*). This desire may seem benign and harmless, but everything that comes from desire has enough power to guide the mind to unfavorable behavior, as Kṛṣṇa warns Arjuna:

> *The man who thinks (of material) objects creates attachment to them. From attachment, desire is created and from desire, anger arises. From anger, fantasy (illusion) arises. From fantasy, confusion of memory (arises). From confusion of memory comes loss of intelligence. Once intelligence is lost, (this man) disappears."* [43]

Desire (*kāma, icchā* or *rāga*) is a difficult enemy to perceive, because it is hidden within us, between our thoughts that we ourselves have created, as a justification for it to become even stronger. The deluded mind is led astray by thoughts that it conceives of, using its own abilities, such as inventiveness or imagination. By assuming a passive and accommodating (tamasic) attitude, appropriate only for the material body, the mind can easily abandon its position as an internal instrument of Puruṣa and become an adversary of the self. A bit further ahead, Kṛṣṇa says:

> *"The higher self should be elevated by the self, the self should not be weakened. The higher self is the only ally of the self and its only adversary."* [44]

The above verse works with a play on words in which the same word '*ātmā*' is used for both the mind (*Jīvātmā*, the lived self) and the higher self (*Paramātmā*). Kṛṣṇa's words highlight the importance of elevating the mind to attain the levity and subtlety of Paramātmā. The true essence of meditation can be seen in this verse, summarized as conquering and preserving a state in which the mind, elevated to the domain of the higher self, becomes its own faithful ally. This achievement, however, must be accompanied by a series of small victories over the challenges that are inherent to this process.

Patañjali, in the yoga sūtras, lists some of these challenges that the

---

[43] Bhagavad Gītā 2.62 and 2.63
[44] Bhagavad Gītā 6.5

mind may encounter along its journey to becoming an instrument of Puruṣa. To simplify Patañjali's teachings, we can consider that he identifies at least three flaws in the functioning of the mind that require special attention from the meditator. The first of these is the mind's tendency to find or create limiting attitudes (*antarāyas*), which it surrenders to at the expense of its own capacity for action. The second flaw is the mind's tendency to doubt its intuition, which brings about disturbances (*kleśas*) to its activities at the expense of the quality of its decisions. The third flaw is the mind's natural tendency to become distracted, or held, by external objects in the course of its activities. These three flaws result in the weakening of personhood if they are not corrected. The Yoga Sūtras, along with other Sanskrit texts, briefly describe these flaws and point to which measures the meditator should adopt so as not to negatively affect the development of their practice.

Patañjali presents a list with nine obstacles (*antarāyas*), which are attitudes assumed by the mind when it is overtaken by the 'tamas' quality. They produce conditions that make meditation difficult: sickness, apathy, self-doubt (insecurity), numbness, inactivity, disinterest, wandering, improper performance and instability[45]. The causes that produce these limitations can be varied, but the result they produce is only one: procrastination.

Procrastination is the postponement of important tasks for insignificant reasons or for no reason at all. Its various causes are almost always based on the fear of taking action or the desire for inaction, especially the attachment to a passive or lazy life, free from a sense of responsibility. The procrastination that we are interested in fighting, however, is not the postponement of just any task, but the postponement of those actions that have the potential to express our true nature, and to reconnect us to our inner self, Īśvara. This procrastination is the worst of all because it takes us away from our center. It weakens our free will and binds us more and more to external objects of desire. It drains our strength, impoverishes our prāṇa and makes presence of mind unattainable. To put it simply, it only disturbs the life of one who aspires to practice meditation.

To resist this type of procrastination, we need to rediscover the source of internal motivation and adopt an active stance that allows us to adjust, in a disciplined way, to our true points of focus. Patañjali says that to avoid

---

45 Yoga Sūtras 1.30

limiting attitudes we need to exercise a single unique nature (*eka-tattvam*)[46]. This gives strength and steadiness to the mind, both in its external, objective focus point, and in its internal, meditative focus point. Referring to the external focus point, he gives us the following information, which helps us to understand what this 'settling of the mind' is (*cittaprasādanam*):

"Or it may come from meditation (dhyānam) on what is desirable." [47]

This is an excellent practical tip that Patañjali offers to help eliminate limitations of the mind. Meditating on something that we like is, in fact, much more stimulating. The mind becomes happy and excited when the subject is precisely what might be called the meditator's 'vocation.' It leaves the illusory comfort of immobility in order to establish a new comfort zone based in activity. Vyāsa broadens our understanding of this point when commenting on this sūtra:

"One should meditate only on that which is desirable. Once stability is achieved there, it is (more easily) achieved on another object." [48]

Patañjali also refers to the inner focus point of meditation, saying that obstacles disappear when the mind surrenders to the command of Īśvara. Indeed, when discussing Īśvara as an internal presence that manifests itself when the yogi speaks the mystical syllable 'Om', the sūtras explain that:

"This is what causes introversion of consciousness and dissolution of the limitations (antarāyas)." [49]

Knowing that Īśvara is capable of dissolving the antarāyas, thus solving the problem of procrastination, makes it even more interesting to better understand who, or what, Īśvara is and where to find it. Fortunately, we don't have to look far to find some very helpful resources. Kṛṣṇa gives the following tips to Arjuna in the Bhagavad Gītā:

"Īśvara sits at the space of the heart of all creatures." [50]

"Even though the higher self (ātmā) is immutable, unborn, even though I am the lord (Īśvara) of creatures, supported by nature itself (Prakṛti),

---

[46] Yoga Sūtras 1.32
[47] Yoga Sūtras 1.39
[48] Yoga Sūtra Bhāṣya 1.39
[49] Yoga Sūtras 1.29
[50] Bhagavad Gītā 18.61

I manifest myself (in the world) through my own force of creation." [51]

These two excerpts from the Gītā make it very clear that Īśvara is the higher self that resides in the heart. It is in the heart, therefore, that the internal focus of meditation should be placed, remembering that, according to the Māṇḍūkya Upaniṣad, this is the space occupied by the highest self, called Prājña - associated with the subconscious and intuition (*prajñā*). With the external focus of meditation placed on vocation, and the internal focus supported by Īśvara's intuition, we can move on to another flaw found in the mind, which also hinders its proper functioning.

At the beginning of the Yoga Sūtras, more precisely in sūtra 1.5, Patañjali identifies a serious problem when he says that the activities of the mind can take place in two different ways, disturbed or undisturbed. He saves this subject for later and only returns to this discussion at the beginning of the second chapter of the Yoga Sūtras. Despite the complexity of the topic, Patañjali manages to summarize it clearly and simply:

"The disturbances (of the functioning of cittam) are: lack of wisdom (avidyā); selfishness (asmitā); desire (rāga); aversion (dveṣa); and the search for belonging (abhiniveśa). Lack of wisdom is the space where other disturbances grow (...)." [52]

Patañjali states here that the mind starts to function in a disturbed way when lack of wisdom manifests itself, bringing with it the other disturbances. We need to learn more about this lack of wisdom if we want to eliminate the disturbances of the mind. Patañjali continues with his explanation in the following sūtra, describing lack of wisdom as a mistaken way of experiencing the world:

"Lack of wisdom is the experience of eternity, of purity, of well-being and of self based on something that is perishable, impure, unpleasant and improper to the self." [53]

The text 'Yoga Vāsiṣṭha' offers a similar description of a mind disturbed by lack of wisdom. Sage Vasiṣṭha explains to the prince Rāma that the disturbed mind...

"...makes the brief become long, finds falsities in that which is true,

---

[51] Bhagavad Gītā 4.6
[52] Yoga Sūtras 2.3 and 2.4
[53] Yoga Sūtras 2.5

tastes sweetness in what is bitter and sees friends in enemies." [54]

Returning to Patañjali, the content of the sūtra cited above may bring up a question that should be addressed. Is lack of wisdom the condition in which we come into this world? Or does this disturbance affect people throughout their lives? Are we born wise? Or do we become wise only as the result of intentional effort? To respond to these questions, we turn again to a comment made by Vyāsa, who says the following:

"The disturbances are five distortions (viparyayās) [of the mind]." [55]

This comment leaves it clear that lack of wisdom and the other disturbances are created by the mind itself. When it is born, the mind is ready to express the wisdom it inherited from Puruṣa, but, for some reason, it loses this privileged condition. The natural condition of the mind, therefore, is one of wisdom, and when this condition is lost, the mind plunges into suffering. But Patañjali reveals a way out:

"The cause of (suffering) that should be avoided is the union (saṁyoga) between the seer and that which is to be seen." [56]

To avoid suffering, its cause must be eliminated, that is, the union between the seer and that which is to be seen. Put this way, it seems as if the mere act of seeing something would cause suffering, which seems unlikely, given the liberating nature of meditation. Deepening our understanding of the concepts of the 'seer' and 'seen' is important here. Vyāsa's comment helps us to better understand what these two components of this undesirable union are:

"The seer (draṣṭā) is Puruṣa, the observer of intelligence (buddhi). That which is to be seen are all of the states (dharmas) that affect the sattvic intelligence." [57]

It should be noted that according to Vyāsa, Puruṣa does not see material objects, but only their essential, sattvic representation, constructed by buddhi in the inner space of the mind. What is actually experienced by Puruṣa is just the subjective image of each object. This experience corresponds to dhyānam, the meditative view of the meaning of the object,

---

[54] Yoga Vāsiṣṭha 3.110.20
[55] Yoga Sūtra Bhāṣya 2.3
[56] Yoga Sūtras 2.17
[57] Yoga Sūtra Bhāṣya 2.17

which is expressed as intuition (prajñā). If this vision of Puruṣa is disturbed by any agitation of the rajas quality, especially that produced by desire, the resulting experience will lack wisdom. The Gītā says:

"This desire, this wrath, which comes into existence through the 'rajas' quality, great consumer (of the mind), great driver of error, know that this is the enemy, in this world." [58]

We can see that the problem here is the natural quality (*'guṇa'*) that prevails in the mind, which can be either limiting (with tamas), agitating (with rajas) or serene and subtle (with sattvam). Depending on the quality that prevails in the mind, the sattvic theater that will be presented for Puruṣa to see may be subject to disturbances by rajas or immobility by tamas, to a greater or lesser extent. In continuing this commentary Vyāsa ponders:

"(...) where did (the conclusion) come from that sattvam is the element disturbed by rajas, the disturber? It comes from the fact that the act of disturbing has the nature of doing (which is the most noteworthy characteristic of rajas). The disturbance (has an effect) on the action of sattvam, not the immutable and inactive Kṣetrajña ('knower of the field', Puruṣa). However, (if) the disturbance of the objective experience arrives in sattvam, then Puruṣa, who receives this vision is also disturbed."

We can illustrate these statements by Vyāsa remembering that the mind can be understood as an instrument (*upakaraṇam*) of Puruṣa. To fulfill its tasks, the instrument must be in good condition. If it were a musical instrument, for example, and it were out of tune, the musician would certainly be out of tune in their performance. No one would say that it is the instrument that is out of tune, but, rather, the musician. Meditation is also an art, and the mind is the instrument of this art. It is exclusively the meditator's responsibility to keep their mind well-tuned to the commands of the higher self.

We will now see a brief summary of the solution that Patañjali offers to eliminate the disturbances that affect the activities of the mind. In sūtra 2.11, he proposes using dhyānam, meditation, to destroy the actions of these disturbances. His method for eliminating these disturbances focusses on combating lack of wisdom - the root of all other disturbances. The

---

[58] Bhagavad Gītā 3.37

description of this method is taken up again starting with sūtra 2.23:

"The union of one's own force (the mind) with the force of the lord (svāmī) is what allows for (the mind) to reach it's authentic state. The cause (of this union) is avidyā (lack of wisdom). The absence of avidyā results in the destruction (of the disturbed aspect) of this union. This is the isolation of sight. The method for eliminating (avidyā) is continued experience (khyāti) accompanied by discernment. Intuition is how we arrive at this method, and we get there through seven different paths." [59]

Patañjali says here that lack of wisdom is what gives rise to the union between the mind and Puruṣa. If this were not so, only the enlightened would have the ability to 'see' the world with the mind, because only Puruṣa has first-person sight. In reality, people whose minds are disturbed by lack of wisdom use this union of the mind with Puruṣa to enjoy life. The sages, however, free from avidyā, use this union to allow for their own dharma to always illuminate their minds. The passage below, taken from Vyāsa's commentary, helps to clarify this point:

"The lord, Puruṣa, is united with that which is to be seen (that is, the inner space of the mind) by oneself, for the purpose of (gaining) this experience (darśanam). Based on this union, having (this experience) of that which is to be seen is enjoyment. But gaining the authentic form of the seer is emancipation." [60]

Patañjali and Vyāsa are saying, in the passages cited here, that the union of Puruṣa with the disturbed mind is produced by lack of wisdom. This same union, but with a mind free from disturbances, has a role to play in the process of transforming the mind. This union makes the subjective enjoyment of the world possible and allows for the mind to acquire characteristics of its own personhood (svarūpam - the *authentic form of the seer*). This means that when authenticity is sought - and this is precisely the most notable characteristic of meditation - it is possible to eliminate lack of wisdom and other disturbances in a special way: with discernment (*viveka*). Discernment spontaneously blocks the external commands that attempt to impose themselves on the meditator's mind, while also strengthening the mind's connection to its unique Puruṣa, Īśvara [61].

---

[59] Yoga Sūtras 2.23 to 2.27
[60] Yoga Sūtra Bhāṣya 2.23
[61] Yoga Sūtras 1.24

The relationship between Puruṣa and the mind that allows for expression of Puruṣa itself is the one that occurs through buddhi (perceptive intelligence) but is only possible when intelligence is pure, that is, when it is recoiled within the realms of the higher self. Vyāsa adds the following words when commenting on this:

"All of the Puruṣas are united with the qualities of nature (guṇas). What is special about this subject is the union of inner consciousness (pratyakcetanam) with one's own intelligence (svabuddhi)." [62]

Discernment has the ability to deactivate all forms of inappropriate intelligence that obstruct the mind's access to its inner command, leaving only the meditator's own intelligence free. This deactivation happens through the elimination of the vāsanās - thoughts derived from external stimuli, habits or memories - leaving the mind free to relate to sensory information with the same enchantment (wisdom) of a child. Vyāsa concludes:

"Is it not true that the simple recoiling of intelligence (buddhi) is liberation (mokṣa)? The recoiling of intelligence arises from eliminating the reasons for not seeing. And this inability to see, characteristic of the binding agent, disappears in the face of true sight. In this case, liberation is the simple recoiling (nivṛtti) of the mind (cittam)." [63]

The true sight (*darśanam*) is that non-sensory sight, which Puruṣa experiences. For this reason, Puruṣa is called draṣṭā - *the seer*. This sight is the foundation of the first-person experience and, in Sanskrit literature, is identical to *prajñā*, intuition. The path proposed by Patañjali to eliminate disturbances of the mind is the elimination of the lack of wisdom. This is done through strengthening discernment, which leads to a life guided by intuition.

Intuition is internal sight, which only manifests when the mind is recoiled into the realm of subjectivity. And here Patañjali identifies another flaw of the mind's operating system: its stubborn tendency to distraction, escaping from this recoiling. It is not for nothing that he defines yoga, right at the beginning of the Sūtras as *"the recoiling of the activities of the mind."* Its purpose is to allow one's attention to be at the service of the meditator,

---

[62] Yoga Sūtra Bhāṣya 2.23
[63] Yoga Sūtra Bhāṣya 2.24

in its proper place, that is, in the central core of the mind. Vyāsa is quick to distill this theme in his commentary on the first sūtra, saying:

"Yoga is samādhi. This is also the natural condition (dharma) of the mind (cittam) in any of its stages. The stages of the mind are: outside itself (kṣiptam), confused (mūḍham), distracted (vikṣiptam), focused (ekāgram) and recoiled (niruddham)." [64]

The literal translation of 'Samādhi' is 'placement with oneself.' It describes an internal effort of the mind that brings the body closer to and integrates it with Puruṣa, making the two become, for all intents and purposes, one. It is a continual effort of the mind, regardless of the stage of concentration it finds itself in. This is why Vyāsa declares that samādhi is yoga, since both are synonymous with meditation, that is, the adjustment of the self to the higher self. Afterwards, he claims that samādhi in the three first stages of the mind, meaning when it is affected by some degree of distraction, is samādhi that is of no use to yoga. Samādhi without focus does not have the strength needed to elevate the mind.

Following the logic proposed by Vyāsa, the mind that is elevated is one that reaches the stage of greatest introversion (or recoiling), niruddham. One must wonder if the movement that elevates the mind is, for the meditator, an inward movement? And if this elevation could result from a search for this recoiling? The answer is yes. Within the magical and subjective space of the mind, the movement that points upward also points inward and toward the center. References to this movement of elevation of the mind are found everywhere in Sanskrit literature. The Śvetāśvatara Upaniṣad, for example, says in verse 2.2:

"With an adjusted mind, we [gain], with the drive of the god Savitā, the strength to reach the celestial world."

The Śvetāśvatara Upaniṣad presents in the seventeen verses of its second chapter the doctrinal rudiments of the meditation process, that is, yoga. The presence of the god Savitā in this verse is not accidental. His name means 'stimulator' and he represents the force that carries the mind upward, 'toward heaven' ('*suvargeya*'). Sāyaṇa, a celebrated commentator on the Vedic tradition, explains that 'Savitā' is the name that is given to the sun when it is hidden below the horizon line. As such, its heat radiates from the earth below, rising toward heaven.

---

[64] Yoga Sūtra Bhāṣya 1.1

The most important and most sacred verse in the whole Vedic tradition, the Gāyatrī mantra, speaks to this same subject, demonstrating the great importance Vedic literature places on the elevation of the mind, which takes place through the process of meditation. Some Hindu sages maintain, based on the traditions of their initiatory lineages, that this verse summarizes the content of all of the more than ten thousand other verses in the Ṛg Veda. The Gāyatrī says:

"Let us meditate on that desirable ardor of the god Savitā. May he drive our thoughts." [65]

The drive of the god Savitā stimulates the thoughts of the meditator to move upward, far from the earth. The material world, with all of its stimuli, draws the mind into the realm of desire, distracting it from its own more elevated purposes. As the mind moves upwards, it also moves inward and away from external objects, and its focus can be fixed on the inner space. It is up to the meditator to prepare the tool, the mind, to be used by the true craftsman, the self that lives within our hearts.

The force that carries the mind out of its inner space is desire. Desire creates strong bonds that 'tie' the mind to perceived objects, producing the illusion that they are needed. The mind is not an entity in itself, as its existence depends on the existence of the body and of Puruṣa; and it is through the mind that these two elements are integrated. The nature of the mind appears to be dual, as if one part were a part of the body and another part were a part of the self, but this duality only exists because the mind is the bridge that integrates these two entities and makes the two become one. One of the upaniṣads describes this dual nature of the mind and explains the reason why it can lead to inappropriate behavior.

"The mind (manas) is said to be dual in nature: pure and impure. Impure, it is motivated by desire; pure, it is free from desire. The mind is the sole cause of human being's imprisonment and liberation. It is classified as 'imprisoning' when it is strongly attached to objects and 'liberating' when it is devoid of objects." [66]

The duality of the mind is defined by its dependent or independent relationship to objects outside of itself. Driven by desire, the mind uses its ability to construct explanations and justifications to feel comfortable with

---

[65] Ṛg Veda 3.62.10
[66] Brahma Bindu Upaniṣad, phrases 1 and 2

each choice that it makes. The meditator's discernment, therefore, needs to be good enough for them to see the real reasons that are motivating their decisions. It is not easy to overcome the rhetorical layers created by the mind when it is agitated by the rajasic quality of desire. For this, a good dose of unattachment and a bit of discipline is needed. Kṛṣṇa says to Arjuna:

> *"Undoubtedly, o Mahābāhu, the mind is agitated and difficult to contain, but with discipline and unattachment, o Kaunteya, it is contained."* [67]

Patañjali repeats the same formula in the Yoga Sūtras:

> *"The recoiling (of the activities of cittam) comes from discipline and unattachment."* [68]

This gives us good insight into the meaning of 'elevating the mind', which can be translated as 'bringing the mind into itself.' Removed from its bondage to desire, the mind settles in a subjective space, a space that Sanskrit literature locates in the heart, and there it finds the peace and discernment characteristic of the sattvic state.

The elevated or inner facing mind is one which approaches Puruṣa, becoming their image and likeness in the natural world. This is something that the mind can only do when its activities are applied to that which is essential to its authentic nature. The mind, if only considered as 'manas', is unable to escape from its innate duality. It needs to integrate with ahaṁkāra and buddhi, the two doors through which Puruṣa and Prakṛti have access to the other's realm - integration that gives rise to antaḥkaraṇam, that is, the mind in its full state.

To better understand this subtle relationship of the mind with Puruṣa, we will discuss the mystery of consciousness in the following chapter.

---

[67] Bhagavad Gītā 6.35
[68] Yoga Sūtras 1.12

9. Consciousness

The troubled connection that the mind builds between the objective body and Puruṣa creates the opportunity for many failures to arise, as we saw in the previous chapter. These failures disturb the functioning of the whole mental system, the main disturbance being avidyā - lack of wisdom. One of the indications that avidyā is active is when *one experiences a sense of self even where it does not actually exist.* In this chapter, we will try to explain how this 'failure' may be the reason why we are able to enjoy conscious experiences. And to understand how this is possible, we need to understand how much we know about that which we call 'consciousness.'

Consciousness is a concept that we accept generically as if it were already well-resolved and thus, we avoid the difficult task of trying to define it. Philosopher Jaegwon Kim describes for us this 'instinctive' perception of what it means to be conscious quite clearly:

> " *'conscious' is just another word for 'awake' or 'aware,' and we know what it is to be awake and aware — to awaken from sleep, general anesthesia, or a temporary loss of consciousness caused by a trauma to the head, and regain an awareness of what is going on in and around us."* [69]

This generic notion that we have about consciousness defines the subject to some extent without, however, clarifying it. The real meaning of 'consciousness' is squeezed into a dark semantic corner of our minds, from where it waves vaguely to those who venture to attempt to decipher it.

---

[69] KIM, Jaegwon. Philosophy of Mind. Taylor and Francis. Kindle edition. (pos. 5830-5832)

Scientists, philosophers, and poets seek, without reaching consensus, the right words to provide an adequate definition for consciousness. But even without being able to describe it with the desired precision, we have created the conviction that it plays an indispensable role in our existence, as Jaegwon Kim explains:

> *"Most of us would be inclined to believe that for all human intents and purposes, a person who has permanently lost the capacity for consciousness is no longer with us. This suggests that consciousness might be a precondition of mentality and personhood— that any creature with mentality must be a conscious being."* [70]

Despite the evident importance of consciousness in our lives, the only discussion of this topic we find in modern thought, until almost the end of the 20th century, are evasive definitions created by philosophers or scientists with the apparent intention of sweeping the problem under the rug. The era of a systemic search for a clear definition of consciousness started accidentally in 1994, at a conference organized by the anesthesiologist Stuart Harmeroff of the University of Arizona (USA). Among the speakers was the Australian philosopher David Chalmers, then just 27 years old, who presented an unexpected (and brilliant) definition for the problem of consciousness. He simply said that it is relatively easy to find physical correlates for almost all mental events, except for the phenomenon of consciousness. For this reason, recognizing that consciousness is the only 'hard problem' in this field of knowledge would be the first step towards arriving at the correct formulation of the characteristics of the object of study. This would allow researchers to start a safe journey toward a solution. In the words of David Chalmers himself:

> *"The really hard problem of consciousness is the problem of experience. (...) It is widely agreed that experience arises from a physical basis, but we have no good explanation of why and how it so arises. Why should physical processing give rise to a rich inner life at all? It seems objectively unreasonable that it should, and yet it does."* [71]

> *"Consciousness is the biggest mystery. It may be the largest outstanding*

---

[70] KIM, Jaegwon. Philosophy of Mind. Taylor and Francis. Kindle edition. (pos. 5834-5836)

[71] Chalmers, David J. The Character of Consciousness (Philosophy of Mind) (p. 5). Oxford University Press. Kindle edition.

The simple acknowledgement of the inherent difficulty in the issue of consciousness constituted a great advancement for researchers in this field of knowledge. The mystery of consciousness is still far from solved and the degree of difficulty of its theoretical formulation is no less than it was before 1994. This redefinition of the approach only gave researchers a new direction, a direction in which they could confidently steer efforts so as to maintain their focus on the true heart of the issue. Since 1994, research on consciousness has gained the respect of the scientific community and of philosophers, and, since then, many interesting theories have been proposed for academic debate.

This very briefly summarizes the modern scenario of research in the field of consciousness. What interests us now is understanding how this subject that is so hard to study has been addressed by Sanskrit literature on meditation. We selected some references taken from the Upaniṣads and other texts, which speak to the existence of three states of consciousness and declare that it is necessary to be conscious in order to exist, while also establishing a dependency of consciousness on the higher self (ātmā).

We begin with a very well-known passage from the Bṛhadāraṇyaka Upaniṣad that is recited by the priest (*prastotā*) responsible for the opening chants of the ritual. Here he represents the mind fearful of the idea of non-existence, making this request to his higher self:

"From nonexistence, make me go to existence. From darkness, make me go to the light. From death, make me go to immortality." [73]

The chant goes on to explain that 'nonexistence' and 'darkness' are the same as 'death', and that 'existence' and 'light' are the same as the state of immortality. True existence, which comes with immortality, is an attribute only associated with the higher self. To experience this attribute, the mind must align with ātmā, the higher self, but first, it must become the materialized version of Puruṣa. It is precisely here that the importance of that 'failure' that we referred to at the beginning of the chapter becomes clear. For the mind to 'transform' into Puruṣa, a change in mentality is needed, an act of faith through which the mind assumes the qualities of the object

---

[72] Chalmers, David J. The Conscious Mind (Philosophy of Mind) (p. xi). Oxford University Press. Kindle edition.
[73] Bṛhadāraṇyaka Upaniṣad 1.3.28

of its attention, even if the nature of this object is inaccessible to it, as is the case with the higher self. It's a small farce, an illusion that is based on that failure in the functioning of the mind, which makes the mind see its higher self where it doesn't actually exist. But there is no other way in which the perspectives of the mind and the higher self could intertwine, if not through the great illusion (mahā māyā), the original source of the material world. Kṛṣṇa says in the Bhagavad Gītā:

"Even though the higher self (ātmā) is immutable, unborn, even though I am the lord of all creatures, supported by nature itself, I manifest myself (in the world) through my own illusion (ātmamāyā)." [74]

"Those that lack intelligence think that I, the unmanifested, have fallen into manifestation, without knowing my supreme, immutable, insurmountable nature. I am not visible to everyone, hidden by yogamāyā. This illusionary world does not recognize me as the unborn immutable being that I am. I know all of the beings that have been, that are living now and, o Arjuna, all of those who are yet to come. However, no one knows me." [75]

The great force of illusion that produced the world also produced consciousness when it made possible the ability to perceive a 'self' in this universe, where, strictly speaking, only 'others' can actually be seen. This magic is made possible because the mind, moved by faith ('*śraddhā*', literally: 'the act of placing the heart'), takes the form of what it believes in. This includes its relationship with the eternal higher self, to whom the mind owes its very existence:

"One who believes that Brahma is nonexistent becomes nonexistent. One who thinks that (they themselves) are Brahma is perceived as existing by others. One who is the embodiment of the higher self (that is, the mind), belongs to the one who comes from the past (that is, Puruṣa)." [76]

This last sentence is repeated a few other times in the same upaniṣad, suggesting that its content is of great importance. It indicates that the mind must submit to the commands of Puruṣa, who is not subject to transformations produced by time. It also reminds us of two phrases from Patañjali's Sūtras which deal with the nature of Īśvara, stating:

---

[74] Bhagavad Gītā 4.6
[75] Bhagavad Gītā 7.24 to 7.26
[76] Taittirīya Upaniṣad 2.6

"Īśvara is a special Puruṣa (...), they are also the guru of the ancients because they are not limited by time." [77]

These statements are found in a part of the Yoga Sūtras that speak to the need of the mind to surrender its command to Īśvara, which, for some who study yoga means a devotional surrender to God. But Īśvara is described as a *'special Puruṣa'*, precisely because it corresponds to that individual instance of Puruṣa, which is the higher self (*ātmā*). The mind needs to connect and subordinate itself to Īśvara in order to achieve full existence. Throughout the process of integration of the two, the universe comes to light and consciousness is born, for the mind becomes a mirror in which Puruṣa, in their role as higher self, glimpses their own existence. The excerpt below describes precisely this creation of the universe from the discovery of the higher self by the self:

"At the beginning of this world, there was only the higher self, in the form of Puruṣa. Having surveyed (the surrounding world), they saw no other higher selves. Faced with this fact, they declared: 'That is me' (so'ham asmi). Thus came the word 'me'." [78]

If the mind is disconnected from this special Puruṣa, it becomes incapable of experiencing consciousness, which is the unique perspective of this 'me.' Delivered to Puruṣa, submissive to their commands, the mind becomes Puruṣa's instrument, it becomes a subjective space and the stage for the theater of consciousness. The space offered by the mind is quite useful, certainly, but only the presence of Puruṣa makes consciousness and the construction of knowledge possible in that space, as Patañjali points out:

"There (in Īśvara) lies the unsurpassed seed of all knowledge." [79]

The seed of knowledge is also the seed of consciousness, which the presence of Īśvara places at the center of our subjective life, in the position of the first-person, the 'me.' As in the plant kingdom, the mind grows and bears fruit from the 'seed of self', reaffirming its existence. In the Bhagavad Gītā, it is Kṛṣṇa who personifies the higher self and Īśvara. This is why he says *"I am the consciousness (cetanā) of the creatures"* [80]. Consciousness (*saṁvid* or *cetanā*) is the condition in which we experience the world from

---

77 Yoga Sūtras 1.24 and 1.26
78 Bṛhadāraṇyaka Upaniṣad 1.4.1
79 Yoga Sūtras 1.25
80 Bhagavad Gītā 10.22

the position of the subject, that is, as *Uttamapuruṣa*, the first-person. Experiences such as feeling pain, making a decision, noticing a color, enjoying the taste of something sweet are impossible to understand if not by living them, that is, experiencing them as a person who feels, thinks, and is present and perceptive.

Consciousness is a condition that manifests itself in the mind only when a coherent connection is established between what the higher self 'sees' with its gaze (*dṛśi*) and that which is to be 'seen' (*dṛśyam*) on the inner stage of the mind. This connection is samādhi, according to what the Haṭha Yoga Pradīpikā says:

"Salt thrown into the water mixes with it and becomes equal to it, because of alignment (yoga). Likewise, the uniting of the higher self with the mind (manas), is called samādhi." [81]

Samādhi, according to Vyāsa, is the natural condition of the mind and comes with some variations, as we saw in the previous chapter. Consciousness, in turn, is a phenomenon that is totally dependent on the existence of samādhi, and, like samādhi, it is also manifested with gradations. Consciousness can vary according to the precision and stability of the subjective focus point, a topic that will be covered in chapter 16.

Consciousness can also vary in state (*sthānam*). Three of these states of consciousness are recognized by the Māṇḍūkya Upaniṣad and are called: *jāgarita sthānam* (awakened state) which corresponds to bodily consciousness; *svapna sthānam* (dream state) which corresponds to mental consciousness; and *suṣupti sthānam* (deep, dreamless sleep state) which corresponds to the consciousness of the higher self that resides in the inner space of the heart. This last state is incorrectly translated as complete unconsciousness, when, in fact, it is a state in which we can perceive the world in the same way as our higher self. In this way, we essentially perceive the meanings of Puruṣa, which are projected in the form of intuitions onto our mental screen. This is the only way we are able to access our higher self that hides within us. The appearance of the higher self to the mind is described as follows in the Muṇḍaka Upaniṣad:

"It is not captured by the gaze nor by the voice, nor by other organs (devas), not by austerity nor by ritual. However, the pure sattvic mind, where the movement of information has been stilled, sees the undivided

---

[81] Haṭha Yoga Pradīpikā 4.5

*through meditation. This tiny higher self can be brought to conscious-
ness right there where the fivefold prāṇa was brought in. The mind (cittam) is the space interwoven by the prāṇas; and in this purified area,
this higher self appears."* [82]

What happens when the higher self appears in this magical space? Consciousness manifests itself, diluted by the three states (awake, dream and deep sleep), adjusting to our personality and building our view of the world. We owe all of this to the great force of Māyā - the illusion that illuminates our mind with the presence of Puruṣa, the cosmic being.

The apparent contradiction that we find here, which makes consciousness a product of illusion, reminds us of modern materialist researchers, such as Daniel Dennett that offer a similar explanation for consciousness. Because they are unable to explain the mind and consciousness in material terms, they choose to deny their existence. These researchers claim that they are only illusions, epiphenomena resulting from the functioning of neurons. Nothing more than an evolutionary accident of nature. But this forces them to consider intention and free will as illusory as well, because all actions that we believe to be deliberate, would be, by the materiality logic, only the pre-determined product of neurological functions and processes. And our will would be just a hallucination that deceives the brain into believing that it is in charge of its own actions.

Sanskrit culture, however, proposes that willpower does exist (*icchāśakti*). As proposed by Sanskrit culture, this willpower would be connected to the functioning of the mind (manas) and would have the ability to introduce changes to the determinism of material nature. We will address this topic in the last chapter of this book. We briefly mention it here just to leave a record of the fact that willpower is real, according to Sanskrit tradition. It is the desire of Paramātmā. When fulfilled, the will of the higher self fills life with supreme meaning (Paramārtha), which is equivalent to the presence of God in the meditator, in the form of enthusiasm. Thus, we can affirm that, from the point of view of Sanskrit texts, *without free and true deliberation, meditation cannot take place.*

Consciousness is sustained by the subjective space of the mind (*hṛddeśa*) within which third-person perceptions (*dṛśyam*) merge with first-person viewpoints (*darśanam*). Consciousness does not exist outside

---

[82] Muṇḍaka Upaniṣad 3.1.8-9

of this space. Nor does it exist if either of its two components is missing - the subject (self) and object (idea). What meditation does is to ensure that these two components are present and connected. This enables not only the manifestation of consciousness, but also its most notable consequence: the lived experience, which is the subject of the next chapter.

10. The Experience

Consciousness is the phenomenon that enables us to open our mind's eye and to know the world, but, ironically, it is itself invisible. It is impossible to observe consciousness. We know that it exists only because we enjoy its resources every moment, when we smell the pleasant perfume of flowers, when we see colors in the objects around us, when we feel the warmth of the sun on our skin, and in so many other situations that we experience in a fleeting moment. This *living*, through which our individual way of becoming conscious of the world is put into place, is what we call 'experience.' Only someone with consciousness is able to have this experience. In this chapter, we will reflect on this experience as one of the components of the meditation process. As always, we will be looking at how Sanskrit literature on meditation, especially Sāṃkhya, introduces this concept in its philosophies.

The most commonly used Sanskrit word for 'experience' is *anubhava*. It is a common term that has been used regularly since the Vedic period and has maintained this meaning to this day. *Anubhava* comes from the verbal root *'bhū'* (to be, to exist, to become) and is endowed with great semantic plasticity. Its capacity for expression can be seen in the paragraph below, extracted from the Praśna Upaniṣad, which deals with the higher self:

"Here, in sleep, this god experiences (anubhavati) greatness. He follows the vision of what has already been seen. He goes after hearing what has been heard. He repeatedly experiences (pratyanubhavati) what has been experienced (pratyanubhūtam) over and over again, in different places and directions. That which has been seen and not seen, heard and not heard, experienced (anubhūtam) and not experienced

(ananubhūtam), that which exists (sat) and that which does not exist (asat), he sees everything, (he is) everything he sees." [83]

The versatility of the concept of experience can be seen here, expressed by the word anubhava and some of its variations. This word encompasses the subjective experience of the mind and the sensory experience of the body as if they were the same thing. The two, in this example, are resolved through the inner, first-person point of view, or sight, the *darśanam*. This is convenient for poetry, but, inadequate for a philosophical doctrine that wishes to establish a clear distinction between perception of a sensory organ and the first-person experience. What the higher self sees was seen first by the eyes and then by the mind, which converted the visual information into an image visible to the higher self. Therefore, according to that upaniṣad, the higher self 'sees' what has been seen by the eyes of the body or the mind's eye, but also 'sees' what these others have not seen: the first-person perspective. The eye sees but does not understand what was seen. The mind shifts through memories in search of images similar to the one it is seeing and finds a position that seems adequate to give this vision context and greater 'visibility,' but the mind is incapable of giving meaning to it's vision. However, just as the cosmic event of a black hole attracts all matter that surrounds it, Puruṣa's 'gaze' attracts all of the informational essence of that vision (darśanam) and, at the same time, projects it's breath of signification onto what it sees. This reveals the way in which Puruṣa, with their understanding, experiences the visibility of the object that was seen.

The experience described by the word 'anubhava' serves to encompass what the eyes saw, what the mind saw and what Puruṣa saw, although these three points of view are conceptually distinct in Sanskrit culture. Puruṣa sees the object in its totality and, at the same time, attributes signification to it that cuts it out of the scenario in a unique way, which will never be repeated. So, to give a very simple and illustrative example, imagine that your eyes see the sky that is rainy and grey, and your mind remembers that today is a dear relative's birthday, thus associating the day with opposite thoughts, of happiness (due to the relative's birthday) and boredom (due to the weather). With this information available, Puruṣa attributes signification to the moment, classifying it as 'happy day' or 'bad weather' or 'uncomfortable' depending on which piece of information they

---

[83] Praśna Upaniṣad 4.5

want to give more emphasis to. With this signification, Puruṣa seeks to express the true feelings that pass through the mind, even if the mind wants to delude itself, believing in a different feeling.

It is not the mind that determines the features of the unique experience enjoyed by Puruṣa. What regulates Puruṣa's experience is discernment, viveka, an ability that only Puruṣa has to separate what is false from what is true. The experience with discernment is the only one that effectively contributes to the success of meditation, precisely because it is the only one that requires the presence of Puruṣa. The master Patañjali certainly realized this, as he searched the vocabulary of the Sāṁkhya doctrine for a technical term to refer to the experience found in the yoga doctrine, limiting himself only to the experience that has the meaning-making presence of the higher self. His search was successful.

The sage who is attributed with the creation of the Sāṁkhya philosophy, Kapila Muni, never composed any scripture. He simply lived according to the principles that he taught and shared his discoveries with a disciple, named Āsuri, who also practiced Sāṁkhya in his daily life. Āsuri, in turn, then taught the secrets of the doctrine to a devoted student, Pañcaśikha Ācārya[84], who composed the original text of Sāṁkhya, now lost, which received the title 'Ṣaṣṭitantram' - 'the theory of the sixty (concepts).' Fortunately, some phrases from this text survived for us to read in the form of citations in other texts, including in Vyāsa's commentary on the Yoga Sūtras of Patañjali. One of Pañcaśikha's phrases appears in the commentary on sūtra 1.4 and it is from this citation that we will be able to examine the concept of the experience that Patañjali found in Sāṁkhya. The phrase quoted by Vyāsa reads as follows:

"Ekam eva darśanam khyāty eva darśanam." [85]
"There is only one vision. Experience is the only vision."

The word *khyāti* is another word used (less frequently) to designate the personal experience, that is, the unique way that each person sees the world in the present moment, serving as the mind's 'gaze' (darśanam). This way of looking at things determines how one lives their life; it guides their understanding and judgement that they construct about themselves and others. The experience includes capturing and storing information that is

---

[84] This lineage is mentioned at the end of the Sāṁkhya Kārikā, in verse 'a.'
[85] Yoga Sūtra Bhāṣya 1.4

converted into experiential (jñānam) or intellectual (vijñānam) wisdom as soon as it gains signification from the higher self. The mind (manas) adds, on its own, a sense of evidence to this knowledge. This means that information that is obtained through experience is treated by the mind as true information, even if it is not.

For the meditator, relying blindly on information originated from a subjective impression in the mind is a sign of lack of wisdom, and can pose a threat to the successful outcome of meditation. But one can't simply be suspicious of everything and try to construct an experience based on a mountain of doubt. A respectful world view establishes wisdom (vidyā) as its main sustaining pillar. For this reason, Patañjali adds an important ingredient of security to this experience: discernment (viveka). He uses in his Sūtras the expression viveka-khyāti - experience with discernment - to describe this antidote to lack of wisdom:

"The method for eliminating (lack of wisdom) is to (maintain) a continuous experience, with discernment. Its limiting term, in seven different ways, is intuition. In the destruction of impurities resulting from the practice of the (eight) limbs of yoga (one can see) the brilliance of experiential wisdom (jñānam) that comes from discernment (viveka-khyāti)." [86]

Through this reasoning about the nature of experience, Patañjali introduces his famous method of the eight limbs. Even before doing this, in the same chapter, Patañjali had already clearly and simply defined what lack of wisdom is:

"Lack of wisdom is the experience of eternity, of purity, of well-being and of self, based on something that is perishable, impure, unpleasant and improper to the self." [87]

With this statement, Patañjali acknowledges the existence of two opposite types of experience: experience with wisdom and experience without wisdom. The difference between them is the presence of discernment, the determining factor leading to better quality thoughts and information produced from each experience. Viveka, or discernment, only manifests when there is understanding, which is an exclusive attribute of Puruṣa. The ultimate goal of meditation, which is to strengthen the inner presence

---

[86] Yoga Sūtras 2.26 to 2.28
[87] Yoga Sūtras 2.5

of Puruṣa, can only be achieved through the continued exercise of experience with discernment. It seems as if Patañjali found here a key element to open the path to the process of meditation, as he himself says:

"Wisdom (jñānam) born from discernment is liberating (tāraka), it achieves everything, in every way and is not subject to the passing of time." [88]

Nothing escapes wisdom constructed with the help of discernment. It is liberating because it protects the mind from illusion and lack of wisdom, leading it towards the realm of intuition, within which Puruṣa can be expressed. The word 'tāraka', translated above as 'liberating' means, literally, 'the one who makes the crossing.' This crossing is a poetic reference to the liberating transition of consciousness, which leaves the third-person perspective to reach the superior condition of consciousness in the first-person (Uttamapuruṣa). This transition in perspective, without which meditation is impossible, becomes complete only when discernment is present, in the moment of enjoying personal experience.

Patañjali states, in sutra 4.29 of the Yoga Sūtras that one who constantly enjoys *experiences with discernment* reaches this samādhi called 'the cloud of dharma' (*dharmamegha*). The Śaṅkara vivaraṇa commentary on this sūtra explains the name given to this samādhi as follows:

"It is called 'the Cloud of Dharma' because from it rains the supreme dharma of kaivalyam."

The word 'dharma' is once again used to identify the conditions that support a particular state of mind, in this case, kaivalyam. Imagine a samādhi, that is, a connection between the mind and Puruṣa, under ideal conditions, in fullness. This is kaivalyam, the ultimate experience of meditation, which, according to Patañjali, is only possible when discernment is present. It is precisely this proximity to samādhi that makes this experience with discernment – *viveka khyāti* – an important component in the process of meditation. The more discernment there is, the more personal the experience becomes, and the greater the quality of the resulting consciousness and samādhi.

As such, in order to obtain the best results from meditation, it is desirable to add discernment to experience. This happens naturally when we

---

[88] Yoga Sūtras 3.55

cultivate the condition of 'sattvam' in the mind, as a calm mind more easily intertwines with Puruṣa. The characteristics of the sattvic mind are described briefly in a part of the Mahābhāratam called the Anu Gītā:

"Happiness, loveliness, nobility, luminosity, well-being, absence of poverty of spirit, lack of impulsivity, contentment, trust, forgiveness, firmness, non-violence, consistency, authenticity, honesty, suppression of fury, suppression of envy, cleanliness, skill and fearlessness." [89]

This passage is part of the teachings passed down by the god Brahmā to great sages in search of final liberation. Practicing these sattvic qualities with dedication and enthusiasm is the same as practicing and strengthening discernment. As a result of this practice, the mind becomes more translucent for Puruṣa's gaze and more receptive to the meanings they see. In short, the phenomenon of consciousness only opens a window in the mind to Puruṣa, but what happens when Puruṣa peers through this window and realizes that there is something 'outside' is what we call 'experience.' When experience is accompanied by discernment, the liberating potential of the higher self is activated and the goal of meditation - kaivalyam - is achieved.

Patañjali's choice of the word 'khyāti' to name the experience that depends on the participation of Puruṣa does not cause him to discard the use of the term 'anubhava', when the topic is, for example, the 'experience' of the sensory perception of objects. This is what we see in sūtra 1.11, which describes one of the activities of the mind, memory:

"Memory is the retention of the perceived object (anubhūta)." [90]

This phrase also serves to illustrate another difference between experience and mere perception. Perception is based on the perceived object, which can be described with relative ease to another person, while experience refers only to the subject who is observing, the 'I.' Experience can only be lived, never shared, because there is no language capable of representing its ineffable nature. Nor can it be modified, as it has no parts, it is not articulated. It is simply a non-verbal understanding that, once acquired, never changes, becoming a foundation upon which thoughts can rest and articulate.

Thoughts partially convert experiences to articulated forms, which can be translated into various forms of expression, especially art. This is

---

[89] Mahābhāratam 14.38.2 and 14.38.3 (Parimal edition)
[90] Yoga Sūtras 1.11

why thoughts can be shared with others, carrying with them small portions of the indescribable experiences on which they are based. Thought is the subject of the next chapter.

11. Thought

Vālmīki, author of the epic poem Rāmāyaṇam, composed another text called Yoga Vāsiṣṭha in which he expands on one of the scenes from the epic Rāmāyaṇam. In Yoga Vāsiṣṭha, he recounts dozens of narratives told to Prince Rāma during his initiation into adulthood. One of them tells of the experiences lived by a brāhmiṇ named Gādhi, who, by grace of the god Bhagavān (Viṣṇu) was able to see the great illusion that sustains the manifested world – the world in which we all live. In response to Gādhi's confusion, who witnesses scenes of a past life as if they were happening before his eyes, Lord Bhagavān explains:

"O Gādhi, it is true (of the illusion) of one who rejects their authentic nature, that their consciousness is unable to see (within themselves) that which illusion expansively sees (around them). Space, stones, ocean, land, direction and everything else, none of this exists 'outside.' This is only in the mind itself (cittam), just as many leaves are (latent) in each bud. Just as fruits and everything else attain multiplicity from the bud, so the earth and everything else attain external visibility from consciousness. In fact, the earth and everything else are in the mind, never outside of it. What is in the bud, however, is what germinates and determines the fate of each fruit. It is the nature of the conscious mind to act at the right time, with attention to the different aspects of the forms (produced), such as the potter who makes and (when necessary) destroys a pot (...)." [91]

Bhagavān's explanation goes on a bit more, but what he says in this passage is enough to inspire reflection about the subject of this chapter: the

---

[91] Yoga Vāsiṣṭha 5.48.48 to 5.48.52

nature of thought. We can clearly see in the text cited above, the framing of external reality as falling within the category of a subjective image produced by the mind. Taken by the illusion of consciousness, the mind ignores its own subjectivity and sees these images as if they were outside of itself. In other words, the mind creates the world in which it itself will be immersed. The concept of a world of ideas allows us to draw a parallel with the theory of Immanuel Kant, who says, criticizing opponents of philosophical idealism:

> *"(...) they have no hope of demonstrating apodeictically the absolute reality of space, because the doctrine of idealism is against them, according to which the reality of external objects is not capable of any strict proof. On the other hand, the reality of the object of our internal sense (that is, myself and my internal state) is clear immediately through consciousness. The former — external objects in space — might be a mere delusion, but the latter — the object of my internal perception — is undeniably real." [92]*

Whether from the point of view of western idealists or from the interpretation of Sanskrit culture, we can say that the whole world seen around us is constituted only by thoughts. Whatever their quality (or reliability), the thoughts we produce are responsible for setting the stage for our experiences and are the only reality to which we have access - a reality created by the mind.

The notable difference between the western point of view and that of Sanskrit literature is that the latter attributes a purpose to the construction of this world made of thought. Indian poets claim that thoughts must faithfully express the authentic nature of the higher self, giving Puruṣa external and internal visibility. At the same time, the higher self fulfills the role of the subject who enjoys these thoughts, like someone watching an internal film, narrated in a language that only they understand. Yājñavalkya says to his wife Maitreyī:

> *"(...) You see, my lady, the higher self is what is to be seen, what is to be heard, what is to be thought, what is to be meditated upon. You see, Maitreyī, it is through the sight of the higher self, the hearing of the higher self, the thoughts of the higher self, the wisdom of the higher self,*

---

[92] Kant, Immanuel. Critique of Pure Reason (Annotated). Kindle edition. (pos. 1294)

The words in Sanskrit used for 'thought' are generally derived from the verbal root *man*, 'to think': *mati* is 'thoughts' and *mata* is 'what was thought.' The meaning of this 'thinking' identified by the root *man* is to 'believe' or 'infer' - referring more precisely to the task of assigning (or guessing) a meaning to the information received. It is no coincidence that the British Sanskritist Monier-Williams traced the linguistic relationship between the Sanskrit root *man* and the English verb *to mean*. Although meaning is produced exclusively by Puruṣa, it is the mind (*manas*) that captures it and gives it visibility in the form of a thought.

Thought has great plasticity, and can take on many different forms, such as of an image (*pratibhā*) or of an expressive sound (*vāc*), of an idea (*pratyaya*) or of a piece of knowledge (*vijñānam*). Thoughts are the primary production of the mind, and what it most enjoys doing. Anything a person is able to do objectively, the mind will have first modeled it subjectively, through thoughts.

In addition to being the creator of the scenery and of the subjective map of the world, thoughts also compose the inner discourse of the mind. They organize personal experience and, with that, build a narrative to support deliberations and actions. This voice that narrates thoughts as they pass through the mind is the craftsman of expression - as it determines the personal way in which we communicate. Everything, in thought, is about communicating and sharing with others. Through our thoughts, we are able to find and occupy our position in the external order of the world. Thought also allows us to follow our inner path, which leads us to discover our natural abilities, that is, our personal dharma (*svadharma*). It's easy to see how learning to control one's thoughts is important to achieve a state of meditative authenticity, as well as to improve one's ability to communicate with others and integrate with the community at large.

It is true that the primary substance of thought is experience, but only thoughts can be shared with another person. Experience, a first-person event, needs to be transformed into a thought in order to be stored in memory. Thought makes the experience an asset that can be retrieved and shared at any time. Experience exists only in the present and cannot be controlled. But thoughts, when stored in memory, can be reproduced and

---

[93] Bṛhadāraṇyaka Upaniṣad 2.4.5

controlled. Memories, in turn, are secondary raw material for the creation of other thoughts. The Sanskrit word for a thought derived from memory is *vāsanā*. Speaking specifically about the vāsanās, Patañjali says:

"The manifestation of the vāsanās is of exactly the same quality as the results (of the actions that produced them). The vāsanās follow an uninterrupted succession due to their connection with memories and habits (even if) separated (from their origin) by birth, place or time. And [the vāsanās] have no beginning, because they are permanent. [Vāsanās] are maintained by [relations of] cause, effect, support and dependance; if these [conditions] do not exist, they [vāsanās] do not exist." [94]

Vāsanās sometimes appear to be thoughts derived from their own free will, especially when they are produced by memories and habits of which, at that moment, we are not aware. It may be the memory of a long-forgotten experience of suffering, or of a moment of happiness from some time in the past to which we cling. It may be the memory of words or acts that affirm our personal or social identity, or it may be just an echo of a belief acquired who knows when. Summoned by these memories, the vāsanās present themselves and force themselves to become the focus of attention, overriding the meditator's desire for peace and tranquility. But the vāsanās cannot be treated as mind-invading aliens, as these thoughts that express old mental habits are the product of our own history - of this life and past lives, according to the Gītā, when it explains what happens to the mind of the dedicated yoga practitioner:

"(...) he is able to find connection with his intelligence from a past life and strives, from there, in the direction of success, o Kuruṇandana. Although he is free, he is taken over by that previous discipline." [95]

Even without being explicit, Kṛṣṇa is surely referring to a 'vāsanā' when he speaks of a discipline (a habit) capable of taking over a person's mind, even though it was created in a past life. It is interesting to note that the person manifesting the vāsanā continues to be free, meaning they are not obliged to continue with the habit that gave rise to the vāsanā. But they do continue. A person's mind just naturally accepts the command of the vāsanā and surrenders to the task of fulfilling it, without any reflection.

---

[94] Yoga Sūtras 4.8 to 4.11
[95] Bhagavad Gītā 6.43 and 6.44

We need to explain, therefore, why the mind is taken by the discipline associated with a vāsanā, renouncing its freedom. And the explanation for this is very simple: the mind appreciates what is true. Truth (*satyam*) is the source of the mind's well-being, according to Mokṣa Parva in the Mahābhāratam:

"So, that which is the truth, that is dharma; that which is dharma, that is light; that which is light, that is well-being. Therefore (also), that which is a lie, that is the denial of dharma; that which is the denial of dharma, that is darkness (tamas); that which is darkness, that is suffering." [96]

The mind detests that which is false because it intuitively recognizes the source of much of its suffering in a lie. So, the mind seeks the light of truth - *satyaprakāśa* - with the goal of recovering its lost well-being. When a vāsanā becomes the focus of the mind's attention, it shines as evidence for the inner gaze, a qualified truth, as the Bṛhadāraṇyaka Upaniṣad says:

"(...) What is seen is certainly the truth! Indeed, what is seen is certainly the truth!" [97]

As the mind can only see its own thoughts, it understands them as real, for the simple fact that they are there, visible. And the mind will continue to believe in these thoughts until some experience makes it see that there are falsities there as well. This is not a problem if we can filter the vāsanās, removing false content from them. Most of the countless thoughts that flow through the mind of an ordinary person are vāsanās. It is possible to assess which thoughts are and which are not vāsanās by following some very simple criteria.

A thought can be a vāsanā if: it is produced based on memory; it anticipates a possible future occurrence; it occurs often; it explains or justifies a past, present or future decision; it depends on the ideas or opinions of others; it is the product of a desire to possess or enjoy material or immaterial goods; it produces bodily tension; it aims to reach some result; it is the result of a fear or aversion.

It is not a vāsanā if: the mind is calm, grounded; it refers to the present moment or is timeless; it results in spontaneous integration of different information; it does not involve bodily effort or tension; the subject only

---

[96] Mahābhāratam 12.190.5
[97] Bṛhadāraṇyaka Upaniṣad 5.14.4

observes the thought without interfering in its dynamics; or it is accompanied by a sense of inner happiness (ānanda).

To filter the vāsanās, one only needs to follow the criteria above and make a sincere commitment to the truth. This is said to be adopting *satyavratam* - the vow of loyalty to truth in perceptions, thoughts, words and actions. Satyavratam is a fundamental requirement for the meditation of yoga; it is one of the five components of mahāvratam (the great vow) that Patañjali borrowed from Jainism and called the *'yamas'*:

"The yamas are non-violence (ahiṁsā), truthfulness (satyam), non-stealing (asteyam), commitment to learning (brahmacaryam), and greedlessness (aparigraha). They are the great vow (...)." [98]

Motivated by the pursuit of well-being, the mind organizes its forces to make a commitment to the truth. Only the truth can sustain the practice of meditation. It is impossible to derive any benefit from a feigned meditation, just as no harvest can be obtained from a feigned crop. A lie, by definition, points to something that does not exist and is incapable of sustaining anything else. There is no victory that can be sustained only by lies.

"Only the truth wins, and not the lie. The divine path stretches along the path of truth, along which the ṛṣis march with their aspirations met, towards the supreme abode of truth." [99]

It remains to be seen how the meditator can be sure that they are cultivating true thought. Most thoughts are created or retrieved automatically without the person even realizing that they are thinking, even when the intention to think is conscious. Thoughts are controlled by the meanings added to them by the unconscious mind. These meanings determine the automatic dynamics that each thought adheres to.

The mind puts excessive faith in its thoughts. Thoughts give the mind a sense of stability that it does not find in the continuous flow of the present experience. Thoughts are there, circulating in subjective space, available, preserved by memory. The mind also trusts its memories and treats them as evidence whenever they appear again in the form of thoughts. However, whatever the thoughts are, they need to be purified by the criteria of their truthfulness for them to express the wisdom of Puruṣa.

---

[98] Yoga Sūtras 2.30 and 2.31
[99] Muṇḍaka Upaniṣad 3.1.6

We have seen in this chapter that, with thought, the mind constructs a subjective world with many luminous and benign experiences for Puruṣa to enjoy. But if the mind is not committed to the truth, this world can become unsustainable, bringing darkness and suffering. The world in which the mind lives is one that it builds itself. Without this world, the mind loses its existence, for it is the only reality to which the mind has access. And without the mind, the world in which we are immersed ceases to exist. Yoga Vāsiṣṭha says the following in this regard:

> "The world is inside the mind, just as empty space is inside a clay pot. With the destruction of the mind, the world ceases to exist. With the destruction of the clay pot, the space inside the pot ceases to exist. For a long time, the hole in the space of the world has been the inner space of the pot in the mind, but it is the nature of this space to find balance by destruction. Take ownership of the shape!" [100]

The mind, with thoughts, gives shape to the world, and what appears to be outside and around us is actually within the inner space of the mind. The meditator who controls their own thoughts takes advantage of the shape their world takes and gains the power to mold their own paradise. The whole world is contained in the mind. But, what about the body?

The material body, which overlaps and lines the subjective space of the mind and establishes the physical boundaries between 'self' and 'other,' is also a reproduction of the mythical universe. But this topic will be saved for the next chapter.

---

[100] Yoga Vāsiṣṭha 5.50.14

12. The Body in Meditation

Imagine how nice it would be if you could practice meditation in a perfect place where no one would bother you, a pleasant place, where you could be at ease, where everything is aligned with your inner nature, an ideal and perfect home for your soul. One who finds a place like this wouldn't want any other place to meditate. They would be satisfied in this place and stay for as long as possible, perhaps for the rest of their life.

You may have already noticed that this place is far from being a fantasy, because it does exist: it is your body. And it is more than just a place to carry out your practices, as it expresses, thinks, and meditates along with you. The objective body can work in harmony with the mind, but for this to happen, the mind needs to settle into the body, integrating with it. With this, our corporeal life becomes endowed with two aspects that integrate and complement each other. The first is the objective aspect, that is, the aspect that gives life to the higher self as a material and perceptible form, that of the third-person.

The Sanskrit perspective teaches us that the objective body is a loan given to us by nature, so that, through it, we can enjoy nature itself. This enjoyment, however, must be carried out responsibly, so that it can be sustained and doesn't harm the connection between the mind and the body. We need to take good care of the body, leaving it clean, detoxified, well-nourished, relaxed; in this way, the mind can function well, and meditation can be successful.

But the body also has a subjective, subtle aspect, which we call the subjective body (sūkṣmaśarīram). It is made up of, in part, the sum of impressions, memories, emotions, thoughts and dreams through which we identify the self that resides within us. On the other hand, the subjective body has features shaped by the conception that we create about our objective body, its states, functions, needs and personality (or personhood), whether it be true or false. The mind is part of the subjective body, and it is nourished, in part, by the same food as the body, as clarified by the Chāndogya Upaniṣad when it says:

> *"Ingested food is divided into three parts. Its densest components become feces. It's medium components, meat. And it's more subtle components, the mind."* [101]

We can see here that the mind can be understood as the most important component of the body, in light of the fact that the raw material used to construct the subjective body are the very activities of the mind. The mind essentially works with information. The way in which the mind organizes and accesses information determines the quality of the functioning of the subjective body, which in turn interferes with the functioning of the objective (material) body.

The subjective body needs us to put in the effort of organization and structuring, so that it does not disturb the proper functioning of the objective body. If we fail to make these adjustments, the subjective body may hinder the enjoyment of the silent observer within us. This effort needed for the correct structuring of the subjective body is found through meditation, which aligns the mind to the higher self.

The body (subjective or objective) is a product of material nature, and, for this reason, it is subject to the same restrictions and capacities that characterize any other material being. However, it is not enough to wait for some automatism from nature for the body achieve its best functioning. Special care must be given to the actions of the body, through aspects such as food, breath, mobility, intelligence in deliberations and other actions carried out by the body.

From the perspective of yoga, the objective body consists mainly of the tamas (dark) quality, which is expressed most clearly in its passivity in response to the commands of the subjective body, the mind, where the predominant quality is rajas (agitation). In the intelligence of the heart, however, sattvam (truth or essence) is the predominant natural quality.

In Vedic times, the rajas quality of the mind was illustrated by an

---

[101] Chāndogya Upaniṣad 6.5.1

image of the sky laden with impurities, mist and dark clouds. The Vedic ritual of sacrifice was practiced with the goal of calming the winds and controlling the rains, so that the land could be cultivated and a path could be opened, making way for the light of the sun and for life. The process of meditation symbolically reproduces this ancient ritual, where the objective body takes the place of the cultivated land, which must be prepared with the careful attention of the cultivator. The mind takes on the role of the sky agitated by the rain and the wind. And the higher self is the knower of the field (*kṣetrajña*), the one who tends to it. We have seen this poetic image of the body as a field for cultivation in the conversation between Brahmā and Śiva in the epic Mahābhāratam that was presented when illustrating the nature of the person (Puruṣa). This idea is also found in the Bhagavad Gītā:

"Sir Bhagavān says:

"This body, o Kaunteya is called the field. One who knows this field is called the knower of the field, by those who have this knowledge." [102]

According to this analogy, which has Vedic origins, a strong connection needs to be made between the knower and the field, between Paramātmā and Jīvātmā, a connection that gives meaning to life in the body. This connection, which is obtained through the path of meditation, is yoga - the adjustment of the 'self' to the higher self (ātmā). We are working here with a connection based on the enjoyment of knowledge, which is only possible through the mind, the subjective body. The mind must be cultivated by the knower of the field so that knowledge can be enjoyed.

Let us try to elaborate further on this information. The mind is the object of action of the knower of the field, which, in the end, is Puruṣa settled in nature [103]. We said before that the mind is the agitated sky and now it seems to have become the crops that will be cultivated in the field (the objective body) for the enjoyment of Puruṣa. The mind can manifest itself in two very different ways: as the agitation of the sky; or as the ordered crops in the soil.

Older Vedic literature celebrates the overwhelming power of the sky, divinizing the heavy monsoon rains in the form of the god Indra, the

---

[102] Bhagavad Gītā 13.2

[103] "Settled in nature, Puruṣa enjoys the qualities born from nature" (Bhagavad Gītā 13.22)

powerful winds as the god Vāyu and the insatiable hunger of fire (the god Agni) that cuts through the sky in the form of lightning. To calm down the agitation of the sky, Vedic rituals prescribe an offering of food to the almighty god, Indra. This food is Soma, the spirit of plants, which has the virtue of mobilizing one of the most mysterious powers of the earth: Uttānapad. The Ṛg Veda (10.72.4) says the following on this topic:

"From Uttānapad, the Earth (Bhū) was born. From the Earth, food was born."

Uttānapad means, literally, 'to fall straight up.' This word designates an ascending force that is found in the body as productive capacity. This is found in abundance in the plant kingdom, where it is called 'Soma.' It is up to the cultivator to calm the skies so that the flow of Uttānapad or Soma may emerge from the earth. By causing Soma to flow abundantly, through plants, the knower of the land makes the skies become benign, converted into biosphere. Only when this happens can we say that the true mind is born, capable of meditation:

"There where the fire is lit, where the wind is controlled, where Soma is released in abundance, that is where the mind is born." [104]

The meditative mind is born this way, by transforming the uncontrolled skies (rajas) into a calm field, full of productive power (tamas and sattvam). Thus, the balanced subjective body is born, bearing the sign (liṅgam) of the presence and command of the higher self. According to the Sāṁkhya doctrine, the term 'liṅgam' translates to the idea of 'significance,'[105] but also expresses the structure through which meaning is revealed, namely, the liṅgaśarīram - the 'signaling' or 'signifying' body.

The liṅgaśarīram, or subjective body, is the embodied expression of the higher self. According to Sanskrit culture, it houses the subtle functions and activities of the mind that correlate with the functions and activities of the objective body, especially those pertaining to the nervous system. Its composition is described as follows:

"Liṅgam is the body overlaid by tanmātras and by more subtle particles." [106]

---

[104] Śvetāśvatara Upaniṣad 2.6
[105] Sāṁkhya Kārikā 5
[106] Sāṁkhya Kārikā Bhāṣya 42

"Liṅgam transmigrates, arising from the (remote) past, independent, self-regulating, (composed of) Mahat and other principles, even tanmātras, unable to enjoy (but) having specific provisions (to express feelings)." [107]

The phrases above explain that the *signifying body* (liṅgaśarīram), or the subjective body, is a structure formed by the three components of antaḥkaraṇam (buddhi, ahaṁkāra and manas), served by the five organs of perception and the five organs of action, and whose limits of action are determined by the five tanmātras.

Following a different approach, Tantric thought brings the characters and landscapes of myths into the objective body, elevating them to the category of microcosm. The 11th century text 'Siddha Siddhānta Paddhati', which introduced yoga to the Nāthas sect, gives us a beautiful illustration of this cultural transformation by presenting a long explanation about the body as a miniature universe:

"The turtle (kūrma) lives on the sole of the foot. Pātālam on the big toe, Talātalam on the tip of the big toe, Mahātalam on the sole of the foot, Rasātalam on the ankle, Sutalam on the shin, Vitalam on the knees and Atalam on the thighs. So is the sevenfold Pātālam under the leadership of the deity Rudra. Nature that shows up as the fury that exists in the body is precisely Rudra Kālāgni.

"Bhūrloka is in the secret place. Bhuvarloka is in the place of the lingam. Svarloka is in the region of the navel. Indra is the deity in these three worlds. Within the body he is Indra, who commands all the senses. Maharloka is at the base of the spine. Janoloka is at the cavity of the spine. Tapoloka is at the stem of the spine. Satyaloka is at the lotus of the root. Thus, Brahma is the supreme deity in this fourfold world. Inside the body, he stays in his authentic form, full of pride and ideas of his own. Viṣṇuloka is in the cavity in the abdomen. There, the deity Viṣṇu is the agent of various activities within the body. Rudraloka is in the heart. There, the deity Rudra is in his own unique form as Ugra ('powerful'). Īśvaraloka is at the base of the chest. That is where the deity Īśvara is, within the body, in his own unique form of satiety. Nīlakaṇṭhaloka is inside the throat. That is where the deity Nīlakaṇṭha is, permanently inside the body. Śivaloka is at the door to the palate. That is where the

---

deity Śiva stays, within the body, in his own unique unparalleled form. Bhairavaloka is at the root of the tongue. That is where the deity Bhairava is, within the body, in his own unique form as the best of all. Anādiloka is in the middle of the forehead. That is where the deity Anādi stays in his own unique form of bliss from the supreme selfness. Kulaloka is at the temples. That is where the deity Kuleshvara is, within the body, in his unique form of happiness (Ānanda). Akulaloka is in the middle of the skull at the lotus (nalini). There, the deity Akuleśvara stays, within the body, in his manifestation of the absence of pride. Parabrahmaloka is at the fontanelle. There the deity Parabrahma stays, within the body, in the condition of complete fullness. Parāparaloka is at the lotus that rises upwards. There the deity Parameśvara stays, within the body, in the dual form of immanent and transcendent existence. Śaktiloka is at the trikūṭa. There the deity Parāśakti stays as manifestation of the condition of creator of everything among all (of the deities). This is how the set of the seven Pātālas and the twenty-one places within the egg of Brahma are considered within the body.

"Brāhmaṇes reside in good conduct, always. The kṣatriyas in heroism. The vaiśyas in determination. The śudras in service. And the sixty-four castes (reside) in the sixty four arts.

"Now, we shall see what is said about the seven seas and seven continents. Jambudvīpa is in the marrow. Śaktidvīpa is in the bones. Sūkṣmadvīpa is in the heads of the bones. Krauñcadvīpa is in the skin. Gomayadvīpa is in the hair. Śvetadvīpa is in the nails. Plakṣadvīpa is in the flesh. These are the seven continents. The acidic sea (Kṣāra) is in the urine. The milky sea (Kṣīram) is in the saliva. The curdled sea is in the phlegm (kapha). The hidden sea is in the lymph. The sea of honey is in the fat. The sea of garapa is in the blood. The sea of the nectar of immortality is in the sperm. These are the seven seas.

"The nine lands are at the nine doors. The land of Bhārata, the land of Kaśmīra, the land of Karpara, the land of Śrī, the land of Śaṅkha, the land of Ekapādas, the land of Gāndhāra, the land of Kaivartaka and the land of the Great Meru. These are the nine lands. Mount Meru resides in Meru himself, Kailāsa resides at the portal of Brahma, Himālaya resides at the back, Malaya at the left side of the neck, Mandara at the right side of the neck, Vindhya at the right ear, Maināka at the left ear, and the Śrī mountain at the forehead. These are the eight main mountains (kulaparvatas). The secondary mountains reside at each of the fingers.

"Pīnasā, Gāṅgā, Yamunā, Candrabhāgā, Sarasvatī, Vipāśā, Śatarudrā, Śrīrātri and Narmadā. These are the nine rivers that reside at the nine (main) nāḍīs. The secondary rivers, creeks and small channels reside at the seventy-two thousand nāḍīs.

"Twenty-seven lunar constellations, twelve Zodiac signs, nine asterisms and the fifteen days of half a month. These reside in the circle of the seventy-two thousand lines on the palm of the hands. Innumerable groups of stars reside in the wrinkles of the fingers. Three hundred and thirty million deities reside in the pores of the arms. Innumerable sanctuaries (of Pārvatī) also reside in the pores. Devas, Dānavas, Yakṣas, Rākṣasas, Piśācas, Bhūtas and Pretas reside in the joints of the bones. The Kulanāgas reside at the chest. Other groups of great ancient sages reside in the pores of the chest. Other mountains reside at the hair of the stomach. The classes of Gandharvas, of Kinnaras, of Kimpuruṣas and of Apsaras reside at the stomach. Other classes of Khecarīs, Līlās, Mātaras, Śaktis and Ugradevatās ('rageful deities') reside in the current of Vāyu (prāṇa). Various clouds reside in the flow of the tears. Infinite siddhas reside in the light of intelligence. The moon and the sun reside in the two eyes. Various trees, vines, bushes and grasses reside in the pores of the hair on the shins. Various worms, caterpillars and flying insects reside in the excrement.

"That which is comfortable (in the body) is the sky. That which is unpleasant is the place of torments (Naraka). That which is action (karma) is imprisonment. That which leaves no alternative is freedom. The awakening of the higher self by the self, in sleep or other states of consciousness, in a condition that gives it knowledge of its own nature, that is peace. As such, universal nature is present in all bodies, the supreme lord, the supreme higher self (Paramātmā), in every effort to preserve authenticity, the one who is endowed with the very form of Cit.

"This is the understanding of the body." [108]

This description, rich in details, shows Tantra's effort to make the space of the body sacred, by drawing over it a mythical meta-geography, which sacralizes it. This meta-geography is the same one we find in ancient texts, located in the hidden space of the heart. The Aitareya Upaniṣad, for example, describes the creation of the universe from the emergence of the

---

[108] Siddha Siddhānta Paddhati 3.2 to 3.14

first-person (Puruṣa), whose body is this mythical space:

"At the very beginning, this world was only the higher self. There was no one else who had seen (it). They thought: 'may the worlds arise.' They gave rise to these worlds: water (ambhas), rays of light (marīci), death (mara) and the waters (āpas). Water is there, beyond the heavens. The heavens are firmly established. The atmosphere are rays of light. The earth is death. That which extends below, are the waters. The (higher self) thought: 'here are the worlds. May the protectors of the worlds (lokapālas) be created. Having thus rescued Puruṣa from being devoured (with the lokapālas), gave them materiality. (The higher self) was hatched. Once hatched, a mouth emerged (from Puruṣa), as if emerging from an egg. From the mouth, speech (emerged), from speech, fire emerged. The two nostrils (emerged). From the nostrils emerged prāṇa. From prāṇa, the wind. The eyes emerged. From the eyes, vision. From vision, the sun. The ears emerged. From the ears, hearing. From hearing, the directions in space. The skin emerged. From the skin, hair. From hair, the herbs and the trees. The heart emerged. From the heart, manas (mind). From manas, the moon. The navel emerged. From the navel, the apāna. From apāna, death. The penis emerged. From the penis, sperm. From sperm, the water (āpas)." [109]

This is how the upaniṣad describes the creation of subjective space, here identified as Puruṣa themselves, into which all deities are transferred. After this happens, the deities sheltered in that mythical space ask the higher self for a place where they can stay and enjoy the food. The higher self offers them the body of a bull, but the deities respond that it is not enough. The body of a horse is refused for the same reason. But when the higher self brings them the body of a person (Puruṣa), they accept it with joy. The higher self then orders the deities to enter the human body to occupy their positions in the natural order. The text goes on to describe details, all very interesting, but we believe that the cited passage illustrates well the way in which the concept of 'body' intertwines with subjective mythical narratives, before connecting with its material form - the objective body.

All these deities that Sanskrit literature describes as if they were integrated with the hidden space of the heart are subjective, poetic expressions of the nature of the higher self. Taken together, they are precisely the force

---

[109] Aitareya Upaniṣad 1.1.1 to 1.1.4

we want to embody with our meditation practice. When we accept the possibility of the supremacy of subjective forces over the ordering of our bodies, and over the outside world, changes are within reach of our decisions
and impediments disappear, as if by magic.

13. The Breath of the Higher Self

Modern thought about Prāṇāyāma can be summed up in a single sentence by Swāmi Kuvalayānanda: *"Prāṇāyāma is the yogic exercise of the breath."* [110] His opinion was the same as other great twentieth-century yoga instructors or researchers, but it leaves out much of the richness found in the vast Sanskrit writings on yoga. When examining older texts, we see that prāṇa is much more than the air of the breath; the magnitude of its importance is almost frightening. The Praśna Upaniṣad illustrates this importance in a passage in which the sage Pippalāda answers questions raised by Bhārgava.

"Venerable lord, how many gods support one creature? How many are needed to make this body manifest? Who is the best of them?

"He (Pippalāda) then answered:

"This space (ākāśa) is a god, the Air, the Fire, the Water, the Earth, Vāc (speech), Manas, Sight and Hearing (are also gods). All of them respectfully salute the one (Brahma) who is to become manifest, saying: we support this body (bāṇam – a stick) which should be erected.

"I can tell you the best of them is Prāṇa: make no mistake! Only I, having separated myself into five selves, can support this body that must be erected.

"They were incredulous. He then marched upwards, as if moved by pride. Where he went, all the others went as well. When he stopped, at that moment all the others stopped as well. It was just like the bees who

---

[110] KUVALAYANANDA, Swami. *Pranayama.* São Paulo: Phorte, 2008. Pg. 37.

follow their king, when he flies upward, all fly upward as well and when the king stops, they all stop. It is such that Vāc, Manas, Vision and Hearing, satisfied with what had taken place, sing praise to Prāṇa." [111]

We can see here the importance given to prāṇa in this text from the Vedic era. It is also clear that the most important attribute of prāṇa is its connection with the control of movement. Therefore, we will start our discussion here with the idea of movement. The common ideas that we have about movement are almost always in association with the idea of moving objects because this is the nature of objective movement, to which our perception is accustomed. Even when objective movement is more abstract, as with variations in an exchange rate, or a sequence of notes in a musical phrase, even then, our mind finds an objective representation for these movements, using graphs, for example.

There are other movements that are only accessible to the subject who observes them, such as, for example, the memory of something that happened, that, for some reason, comes to mind. This type of movement, which occurs through images in the mind, can be considered subjective. There are also subjective movements that are more abstract, so much so that the mind is unable to associate them with any sort of object. These movements are, for example, mathematical vectors, or the meaning of speech, or words, which move the mind toward a meaning that never fully reveals itself, in a *'becoming'* that never fully materializes.

Objective or subjective, concrete, or abstract, all of these movements are just prāṇa carrying out its activities, which extend into the instrumental realm of the mind (antaḥkaraṇam). The Haṭha Yoga Pradīpikā states the following about the relationship of prāṇa with the mind:

"In the movement of the breath (vāta, that is, prāṇa), the movement of cittam should arise. In the immobilization (of prāṇa), the immobilization (of cittam) should arise: the yogi achieves stability and then the breath can be recoiled." [112]

The recoiling of prāṇa is the recoiling of the activities of cittam, which are then controlled by the meditator.

"Only he who controls the breath controls the mind, and only he who

---

[111] Praśna Upaniṣad 2.1 to 2.4
[112] Haṭha Yoga Pradīpikā 2.2

controls the mind controls the breath." [113]

For this statement to make sense, prāṇa needs to have some role in the structure of the mind (cittam). The activities of prāṇa and manas need to be aligned with each other, in order for prāṇa to participate in the changes that occur within the mind. And it seems that the Bhagavad Gītā refers to just this when Kṛṣṇa says:

"The stability through which the activities of the mind (manas), prāṇa and the senses are maintained in correct alignment, this stability is called sattvic." [114]

The Sanskrit word used to mean 'mind' in this verse is 'manas,' that is, one of the three components of the mind as an internal instrument (antaḥkaraṇam). The other two components, to which manas must firmly align are buddhi and ahaṁkāra, but the above verse replaces them with prāṇa. And the Gītā is not alone in this concept; it is actually possible that Gītā inherited this idea from the Muṇḍaka Upaniṣad, which states the following:

"From Puruṣa are born prāṇa, manas and all of the indriyāni (...)" [115]

Although these phrases seem to reveal an opinion that differs from the one presented by Sāmkhya, which describes the mind as a result of the combination of manas, buddhi and ahaṁkāra, it is possible that what we find here is an older concept of the nature of prāṇa. In order to arrive at a better understanding of prāṇa occupying the positions of buddhi and ahaṁkāra, it serves us well to examine two other textual references in which manas and buddhi form a trio with the higher self (ātmā), which appears in the place where Sāmkhya would place ahaṁkāra:

"The senses (indriyāni) are of an elevated nature. The mind (manas) is superior to the senses. Intelligence (buddhi), however, is superior to the mind. But they, (the higher self) are superior to intelligence!" [116]

"Beyond the senses (indriyāni) are the meanings (arthās). Beyond the meanings is manas. Beyond manas is buddhi. Beyond buddhi is the great ātmā. Beyond the great (ātmā) is the non-manifested (ātmā). Beyond the

---

[113] Haṭha Yoga Pradīpikā 4.21
[114] Bhagavad Gītā 18.33
[115] Muṇḍaka Upaniṣad 2.1.3
[116] Bhagavad Gītā 3.42

non-manifested is Puruṣa. Nothing is beyond Puruṣa. This is the limit. This is the ultimate movement (gati)!" [117]

These last two quotes taken together show that ahaṁkāra can be considered to be the manifested ātmā, and that, beneath ahaṁkāra, intelligence (buddhi) is always there, able to connect with ahaṁkāra. The resulting pair, ahaṁkāra-buddhi or ātmā-buddhi, is identical to prāṇa. Taking into consideration the model developed by Sāṁkhya, this pair (that is, prāṇa) joins with manas to provide body to the mind as an internal agent (antaḥkaraṇam or cittam) and it, connected to the senses (indriyāṇi), completes our cognitive structure.

In view of the strong relationship of prāṇa to movement, we can translate buddhi and ahaṁkāra as the two fundamental movements of prāṇa, the inhalations and exhalations of a subjective breath within the mind. Ahaṁkāra is the movement of inhalation (apāna) of the higher self and buddhi is the movement of exhalation (prāṇa) of the higher self. Both are endowed with the nature of the higher self, of ātmā, for which buddhi and ahaṁkāra are like the entrance and exit doors of material nature. It is easy to conclude that prāṇa is the form assumed by ātmā when they enter the universe of the third-person, the universe of manifestation. The Praśna Upaniṣad confirms this by saying:

"this prāṇa is created from ātmā" and *"this ātmā is in the heart (hṛdi)."* [118]

The Kauṣītaki Brāhmaṇa Upaniṣad defines prāṇa even more precisely and succinctly:

"Prāṇa is Brahma." [119]

The Bṛhadāraṇyaka Upaniṣad confirms this statement:

"Who is the one god? Prāṇa. He is the one Brahma." [120]

Understanding this information correctly is an important task for the meditator since prāṇa, identified as buddhi and ahaṁkāra, corresponds to two thirds of the structure of the mind - the instrument (and object) of meditation. And, having been associated with the higher self (ātmā or Brahma),

---

[117] Kaṭha Upaniṣad, vallī 3, phrase 10
[118] Praśna Upaniṣad 3.3 and 3.6
[119] Kauṣītaki Brāhmaṇa Upaniṣad 2.1
[120] Bṛhadāraṇyaka Upaniṣad 3.9.9

prāṇa can prove to be the strong link that connects the first-person perspective with that of the third-person, inside the mind.

We have already seen that prāṇa expresses itself as movement, and now it is important to clarify what exactly it is that moves into and out of the mind or remains inside of it. The natural response is 'information' since the mind deals with information all the time. Objective and subjective information is the raw material of the activities of the mind. These two kinds of information are continuously pulled by the movement of prāṇa.

Objective information originates from sensory impressions (*pratyakṣa*), that are collected by manas, combined with each other, and carried toward the higher self (ātmā) by apāna (inhalation, equivalent to ahaṁkāra) becoming experiences. Subjective information is brought from the higher self by the exhale, prāṇa (equivalent to buddhi), to the inner space of the mind in the form of meanings that are delivered to manas, which, in turn, manifests them as intuition (*prajñā*). Intuition, therefore, is an interference of prāṇa in manas, resulting in meaning connected to the sensory impressions that initiated the process, thus creating a symbol or word. According to this model of how the mind works, manas is unable to process the input of information without the presence of prāṇa. Without prāṇa, there is no inner vision, there is no intuition.

The strong connection between prāṇa and intuition that is born from the higher self is explained in a passage of the Kauṣītaki Brāhmaṇa Upaniṣad, in which the god Indra (the ruler of the gods) converses with the sage Pratardana. Indra represents the mind leading the 'devas' - which represent the organs of action and perception (*indriyāṇi*) - and, as such, recognizes that their attributes are due to prāṇa. Indra says to Pratardana:

"I am prāṇa. Think of me as the higher self of intuition (Prajñātmā), as immortality and as life (āyus). Life is prāṇa. Prāṇa is life. Only prāṇa is immortality. As long as prāṇa inhabits this body, there is life. Only through prāṇa can immortality be attained in this world. Through intuition (one attains) true comprehension (saṁkalpa)(...)." [121]

"(...) That which is prāṇa, that is intuition (prajñā). That which is intuition, that is prāṇa. (...)." [122]

In these phrases, prāṇa is identified with Prajñātmā ('the intuitive

---

[121] Kauṣītaki Brāhmaṇa Upaniṣad 3.2
[122] Kauṣītaki Brāhmaṇa Upaniṣad 3.3

self'), which is equivalent to the concept of Paramātmā, the self that resides at the heart. The breath of the higher self is this movement of prāṇa carrying information in and intuitions out of the inner space of the mind. Its *inhale* (apāna) is the centripetal movement of information that arrives from outside through the senses, and which is carried to the self in the form of first-person experiences. Its *exhale* is the centrifugal movement of information that gives personal meaning to the experiences and to the sensory setting. When they reach the organs of action, the meanings of the exhale give form and substance to the objective body and to the mind. The breathing of the higher self occurs without interruption, and even in moments of deep sleep information continues to travel the material or subtle paths of the body. Its absence signals death of the body or of the mind. Information can be moved or immobilized consciously and intentionally, or, more often, unconsciously, driven by habits, memories and desires.

There is one caveat, however. Intuition is not necessarily a reliable source of information, as it can carry improper meanings into the mind. Although according to Sanskrit culture the source of intuition is Puruṣa, this does not guarantee that it will be received correctly by the mental structure, since this mental structure can be affected by various disturbances. Contradictory intuitions can arise in the mind and collide with one another, provoking confusion and doubt.

Imagine that one day you decide to take a walk through the streets and notice that there are clouds in the sky, meaning, it might rain. Because you are sure you want to walk, you have to decide whether or not to bring an umbrella. Your intuition says there is no danger of getting wet and you decide to leave the umbrella at home. At the door, you notice that other people passing by are carrying umbrellas. Another intuition comes to mind, saying that you should probably take your umbrella too. The intuitions collide and you decide to take the umbrella, to be sure you stay dry. Then you remember that you left the umbrella in the trunk of your car, and your intuition that it is not going to rain is strengthened by laziness at the thought of going to get it. In the end, you leave without the umbrella and, of course, it rains. When it does, you think: *"I knew this was going to happen..."*

This conflict of intuitions happens all the time in the mind that has not yet found a firm intuition that prevails over the others. Two or more opinions vie internally for attention, raising arguments and justifications in their own favor. While the decision is pending, the mind shifts its attention between visions without stopping at any one of them. Patañjali credits the multiplicity of inner visions to the multiplicity of mental nuclei that populate the subjective body, although only one of these nuclei has the ability to definitively stop this dispute between them:

"The goal (which one wants to achieve) does not lead to material activity, but to the interruption of the process of choosing. That is why there is the knower of the field (the farmer). The mental nuclei (cittāni) are created exclusively from selfness (asmitā). A single cittam among many leads to the interruption of the action (of choosing). There (in this cittam) born from meditation (dhyānam), there is no repository (of actions)." [123]

It is as if, instead of just one mind, there are many other minds within the same person. A cittam, or mental nucleus, is created in the movement of the inhalation of prāṇa if the seed of a future action has been planted by manas in the inner space of the mind. The movement of the inhale, which has the nature of *asmitā* (or *ahaṁkāra*) gives this action an agent - the 'I' - which, being the same for all of the other nuclei, eliminates the feeling of multiple personalities. The movement of the exhale, which has the nature of buddhi, awakens in the newly created nucleus the intelligence of the farmer, who is the knower of the field (*kṣetrajña*), that is, Puruṣa.

Thinking now of the set of nuclei created by the functioning of the mind, it is clear that they do not act in isolation, but as a collective body. In the movement of the exhale of prāṇa, personal meanings are commanded by the mental nucleus (cittam) that has the greatest power of command over the other competing mental nuclei, for the matter at hand in that moment. Supposing the best hypothesis, in which the mind is free from attachment and other disturbances to its functioning, the strongest nucleus will also be the closest to the higher self of the heart (Prajñātmā or Paramātmā) and, in that case, the result would be reliable intuition. Actions resulting from the strengthening of this mental nucleus closest to the self of the heart will be sustainable, consistent with the individual's personal dharma. That is why the person is not imprisoned by the results, good or bad, of their actions. This is the natural make-up of the liberating mental nucleus to which Patañjali refers as the 'only cittam within many' - the only one capable of recoiling the activities of the mind, which are then able to enter a state coherent with samādhi. This cittam is established only when manas

---

[123] Yoga Sūtras 4.3 to 4.6

gives over its attention and command to Īśvara; only then the purity of this mind is equal to the purity of Puruṣa.

It is worth noting how Sanskrit culture values personhood in the circulation of information in the inner structure of the body and the mind. The personal meanings driven by the exhalation of prāṇa are necessary to maintain coherence, integrity and to build individual identity. Its intuitive manifestations reveal to the meditator glimpses of their own dharma.

Impersonal meanings are also needed for us to understand and accommodate information brought by others into the mental setting. They constitute a repertoire of shared signals that enable us to exchange information with other people, or even with nature itself. Without them, there is no communication or dialogue and comprehending the viewpoint of the other is impossible. These impersonal meanings join the set of cognitive resources that we have available, brought by the mental nuclei (cittāni) that, within the mental setting, represent the interests of others. The only problem with these aggregated meanings is the fact that they are also pulled by prāṇa into and out of our mental center, bringing the risk of confusing, in our mind, what is personal content with what is aggregated content.

Prāṇa continually moves the meanings offered by the higher self (Puruṣa) toward the fragmented information that comes from the external world, brought in by the inhalation of apāna. But it is nature (Pradhānam) that materializes information and meanings in the forms suitable for each purpose, inside or outside our body.

Prāṇa, just another name for ahaṁkāra and buddhi, plays the role of the two-way path that connects Puruṣa to Pradhānam. It creates a kind of 'vectorial' resonance between the two through which it provides intensity and meaning to material activities. Interruption of these two perceptible movements corresponds to the stillness of prāṇa – the third Prāṇāyāma. Patañjali says:

"Out, in and stillness (stambha), those are the activities (of prāṇa)." [124]

If prāṇa is interpreted as pure movement of information, this stillness of the third Prāṇāyāma exists permanently because the movements inward and outward continuously coexist and never actually come to an end.

---

[124] Yoga Sūtras 2.50

They are an eternal *becoming* in which opposites meet and nullify each other without ever losing their integrity. In the following sūtra, Patañjali says that the fourth prāṇāyāma creates a realm that integrates the space outside with the space inside. In this realm, located within the subjective space of the mind, a magical integration between information and meaning occurs, through which the two irreconcilable universes become one. In the grammatical world, verbs (words that express movement) are the element in which the perspectives of the first- and third-person are found, and discourse is the abstract space in which these perspectives inflect and integrate harmoniously.

Control over movement of internal meanings and their connection with information coming from the external world is prāṇāyāma. Actual control over this movement of prāṇa depends on the meditator's capacity for visualization, even if they are able to experience indirect control through breath practices. Through breath practices, when we lengthen one of the phases of the cycle, we stimulate the corresponding phase of the breathing process of the higher self. The exhale intensifies meaning. The inhale intensifies attentiveness and, with it, the quality of information that is extracted from the experience. The pause (or stillness) of the breath stimulates the attribution of meanings to information, giving meditation a more strongly intuitive character.

For a good meditator, control over meanings is a key element for increasing behavior of the mind and the health of the body. But literature on meditation also speaks to another important component: food. This is the topic that we will discuss in the next chapter.

14. Food in Meditation

Food is everything that provides us with the nutrients we need to maintain growth, structure, and life. For nutrients to be extracted from the food we eat, we need to disassemble them through digestion, to then assimilate and convert them into components which will become a part of our organism. Good quality food is one of the foundations for the correct functioning of the body, which, in turn, gives us the physical correlates of our mental life. This is where food and the process of meditation cross paths.

Sanskrit culture includes dietary discipline as part of the meditation practice. We think with the mind and with the body, simultaneously, and therefore, we need to take good care of our bodies. A mistreated body impairs the activities of the mind, which makes it more difficult for the higher self to manifest, which is, as we know, the end goal of meditation. Kṛṣṇa discusses this with Arjuna:

"Those who indulge in a violent asceticism, not prescribed in the scriptures, connected to a false selfness, carried away by the force of desire and passion, senseless, weakening all components of the body, and of myself that am within the body, know that these (people) are demons, without a doubt." [125]

In the verses that follow, Kṛṣṇa speaks briefly about food, which is described according to three categories, corresponding to the three types of faith that the meditator can choose to sustain their deliberations. Each type of faith is linked to one of the three qualities of matter - sattvam, rajas or

---

[125] Bhagavad Gītā 17.5 and 17.6

tamas – and thus are the three categories of food.

These references from the Bhagavad Gītā to food are repeated in some of the Sanskrit literature on yoga, indicating unexpected importance of this subject in the context of meditation. The references seem to say, at first glance, that to meditate correctly, the body must be nourished correctly. The Haṭha Yoga Pradīpikā, in verse 1.59 gives the same importance to control over food (mitāhāra) as to renunciation (tyāga) and commitment to learning (brahmacaryam). It then declares:

"A light and pleasant meal, reduced by a quarter, enjoyed for the satisfaction of Śiva, is called mitāhāra." [126]

We can see here that the main goal of mitāhāra, a balanced diet, is to satisfy Paramātmā (here called by the name of the god Śiva) and not merely to nourish the body. Certainly, food that satisfies Paramātmā is of a different nature from that which only meets the needs of the body, and it would be very useful if this were explained more clearly in the Sanskrit text itself. Pradīpikā, however, only says that the yogi should eat light and enjoyable foods, which it describes briefly. [127] According to the Gītā, [128] these foods are connected to the sattvam quality of matter, but it seems unlikely that this material food will interest or please Paramātmā in any way.

We can examine this topic in another way. The word āhāra (meal or food) means literally 'the act of taking for oneself' or 'appropriation' and relates directly to the word pratyāhāra (the recoiling of the senses), which can open up the possibility of a conceptual connection between food and meditation, through the sensory organs. To follow this train of thought, we need to find references in Sanskrit texts that confirm one of the following two hypotheses:

a) There is more than one type of food and one of them relates to sensory stimuli; or
b) The meaning of the Sanskrit word for 'food' can be expanded to something that goes beyond material nourishment of the body.

Chapter 15 of the Bhagavad Gītā presents the multiplicity of the kinds of food that exist, as Kṛṣṇa explains to Arjuna, after describing his own brightness, which comes from the sun and is in the moon and in the fire:

---

[126] Haṭha Yoga Pradīpikā 1.60
[127] Haṭha Yoga Pradīpikā 1.64 and 1.65
[128] Bhagavad Gītā 17.8

"Having become Vaiśvānara, sheltered in the body of living beings, with balanced prāṇa and apāna, I digest the four types of food." [129]

To our disappointment, however, Kṛṣṇa takes it for granted that Arjuna knows what these four types of food are and says nothing more about them. Once again, the task of discovering what the types of food are falls to us. Ādi Śaṁkarācārya, when commenting on this verse of the Gītā, informs us that the four types are those that are swallowed whole, those that are chewed, those that are sucked and those that are licked. This explanation from the great sage, however, does little to help us in the effort to discover what food satisfies Paramātmā. We need to find more information in other literary sources, using the reference in the Gītā to Vaiśvānara, the internal fire of our body, as a starting point.

We have mentioned Vaiśvānara before, in the chapter about the four-fold nature of the person, where we stated that vaiśvānara is the self found within the body. It is also another name for the god of fire, Agni, who, within the body, is the instrumental agent of digestion. The concept of digestion, within Sanskrit culture, is rich in meaning. The term *āhāra-pāka* for example, is used for digestion of common food, promoted by gastric fire (symbolized by the god Agni). *Pāka* mean digestion, but it also means to cook, that is, the preparation of food by fire. *Pāka* also means transformation that leads to ripening - *phala-pāka*, for example, is the ripening of a fruit. Just as digestion is produced by fire, it is also similar to the ritual of sacrifice *yajña*, in which the food offered to the gods is thrown into the fire. For this reason, the god of fire is also called *Devavaktra* ('the mouth of the gods') because this is how food is offered for the enjoyment of the gods. Departing slightly from the pattern, the word *karmavipāka* is used for the digestion (ripening) of actions. [130] This term suggests that a person can also be nourished and strengthened by taking correct actions, which affect the body and spirit simultaneously. All of the information that enters on the breath of the inhale of the higher self, all enjoyment, serves to feed Paramātmā. The text below, taken from the Kaivalya Upaniṣad, reaffirms this same idea, which links nourishment of the body to the enjoyment experienced by the self:

"That higher self deluded by Māyā makes a whole body to (cover) its skeleton. With women, food, drink and various pleasures, he attains

---

129 Bhagavad Gītā 15.14
130 Yoga Sūtras 2.12 to 14

satisfaction when in a waking state (jāgrat)." [131]

There is a verse from the Bṛhadāraṇyaka Upaniṣad (1.3.17) that says that prāṇa ritually chanted to its own food - that is, produced it with mantras - and then ate it, because whatever the food, whoever eats it, it is prāṇa. And the next verse says that everything in this world that is food belongs to the higher self (ātmā). Once again, we see an idea expressed here that we discussed in the previous chapter, where prāṇa and the higher self are identical and are the only enjoyers of food. The same Upaniṣad also says:

"This world is only food and those who eat food. Soma is the food and Agni is the devourer of the food." [132]

"Food is eaten by the voice, indeed." [133]

"Who are the two gods? They are food and prāṇa." [134]

Prāṇa creates food, which is the world itself. Therefore, it is the action of prāṇa, the movement of the exhale of ātmā, that creates the world. And after that, prāṇa itself, in the movement of the inhale of ātmā, enjoys the food that it has created. The feeding cycle thus becomes an instance of prāṇāyāma. Vedic texts reveal a great respect for enjoyment, when the enjoyer is ātmā. The Īśāvāsya Upaniṣad says, in its first verse:

"This whole world is for the enjoyment of Īśa, whatever its life form (jagat) on earth (jagatī)."

The word 'Īśa,' which means 'god', is a synonym for Īśvara. It is used to designate the higher self, ātmā. This confirms the idea that even enjoyment through the body has the purpose of serving the higher self. We encounter here, however, a question related to this enjoyment of the higher self. According to the Māṇḍūkya Upaniṣad, there are three instances of the higher self within us: one for the body, one for the mind and one for the heart. The Maitreyyupaniṣad calls them Bhūtātmā, Pratyak and Paramātmā. The question, then, is: *which one of the three should enjoyment serve?*

Paramātmā is the immutable higher self, the Parameśvara that resides

---

[131] Kaivalya Upaniṣad 12
[132] Bṛhadāraṇyaka Upaniṣad 1.4.6
[133] Bṛhadāraṇyaka Upaniṣad 2.2.4
[134] Bṛhadāraṇyaka Upaniṣad 3.9.8

in the lotus hidden within the heart.[135] Pratyak means 'inner' or 'facing backward', carrying a suggestive similarity to antaḥkaraṇam ('internal instrument'), that is, the mind. In other texts, Pratyak, the self of the mind, is called Jīvātmā. Bhūtātmā is passive and obedient to the commands of Jīvātmā. Yoga uses the concept of Jīvātmā to align with Paramātmā; the Haṭha Yoga Pradīpikā says:

"The similarity and unity of both Jīvātmā and Paramātmā (...) is called samādhi." [136]

We don't eat just to give sustenance to the body, but to ensure that the body provides the support needed to sustain the mind-to-ātmā (or Jīvātmā-to-Paramātmā) connection. This is the main purpose of food: to provide support and quality to cognition, and, as a result, to meditation. In the Sanskrit understanding, food is not only what we ingest and digest to sustain our bodies. It is also the information brought into the body via the sensory organs. It is also each of our accomplishments and their consequences. It is also the thoughts that build up in our mind and that, as if they were offerings to Puruṣa, need to be purified by the fire of ritual sacrifice, which, within our bodies, is also the digestive fire. Kṛṣṇa says in the Gītā:

"Better than the sacrifice of material goods is the sacrifice of knowledge, o Parantapa. Every action, without exception, o Pārtha, resolves itself in knowledge." [137]

Prāṇa creates food by giving meaning and significance to it, turning it into something that can be known or into knowledge itself. Afterward, prāṇa consumes the food, giving it body and movement, converting knowledge into action. Prāṇa sacrifices knowledge (food) by casting it into the fire, which represents the continuous movement of transformations. The whole world is food created for the enjoyment of the lord, which is inevitably destroyed by the very fire of the enjoyment of the lord. At the end of this digestion-transformation, only the meaning of the food remains, that is, perishable knowledge is destroyed and transformed into understanding. Since food is a product of prāṇa, which is the breath of ātmā, we can conclude that understanding (or meaning) is the purest food that exists, as it comes directly from ātmā. The purity of food is a subject that

---

135 Maitreyyupaniṣad 1.12
136 Haṭha Yoga Pradīpikā 4.7
137 Bhagavad Gītā 4.33

comes up often in Sanskrit texts, since the Vedic period, as can be seen, for example, in the Chāndogya Upaniṣad:

"In the purification of food (āhāraśuddhi) is the purity of sattvam. In the purity of sattvam is steadfast memory. In the restoration of immutable memory is the liberation of all of the knots." [138]

Patañjali, who certainly had in-depth knowledge of the upaniṣads, shows the importance of the *purity of sattvam,* mentioned in the passage quoted above, when he says:

"Kaivalyam arises from the equal purity of both sattvam and Puruṣa." [139]

Kaivalyam, which is the ultimate goal of the meditator, depends on the purity of sattvam to be equal to the purity of Puruṣa. Any speculation that supposes the existence of impurity in Puruṣa is out of the question. They are pure by definition, as the source of consciousness and the first-person experience. But the upaniṣad warns that the purity of sattvam depends on the purity of food. We have seen what we call food in the literature on meditation can encompass a wide variety of things beyond that which we ingest to nourish the body. The purity of food, therefore, is that which we obtain when we select the words we use, the information we collect, the actions we promote and the meanings we attach to all of these. All of this makes up our mental digestion and must be adjusted to our most authentic nature in order to be considered pure.

Let us now try to understand what this *purity of sattvam* is. Antaḥkaraṇam is contained in Pradhānam and is therefore subject to the dynamic of the three characteristics of matter in nature - tamas, rajas and sattvam. The mind, in the course of its activities, can assume any of these characteristics. When the tamas quality is predominate, the mind adopts a passive and receptive attitude, which connects it more strongly with the characteristics of the material body. This tamasic attitude is useful when we need to receive new information, in the context of learning, for example. When the rajas quality is predominate, the mind adopts a reactive and creative attitude, which keeps it within the characteristics of its own mental nature. This rajasic attitude is more suitable for processing and 'digesting' incoming information. And when the sattvam quality is predominate,

---

[138] Chāndogya Upaniṣad 7.26.2
[139] Yoga Sūtras 3.56

the mind adopts an attitude of withdrawal and sublimation that connects it directly to the higher self of the heart. The sattvic attitude of the mind is the only one that is important to be maintained during the meditation process. This is why meditation literature sometimes uses the expression '*purity of sattvam*' to mean '*purity of the mind in the sattvic state.*' If this is not clear on its own, Vyāsa adds the following in his commentary:

> *"When the 'essence of intelligence' (buddhisattvam) becomes free from the impurities of rajas and tamas, reduced to the conviction that it is different from Puruṣa and with the seed of disturbances having been destroyed (by fire), then (intelligence) enters into a state of purity similar in nature to that of Puruṣa. So, the purity of Puruṣa is the absence of enjoyment on the part of the one who has been served (the intelligence of the mind)."* [140]

Among its many tasks, the mind is responsible for connecting a meaning to each object. This link that the mind creates between an object and its meaning is called 'yoga,' in Sanskrit grammar. The grammatical concept of yoga includes the attribution of meanings to food. It is possible to eat with the intention of giving pleasure to the body, or of satisfying the desire to eat, or even to become inebriated, and all of these are meanings given to food that make it an obstacle in the search for a lighter, more sattvic mind, one that is more suited to the process of meditation.

But it is also possible to give food the task of nourishing the mind to make it more sensitive, responsive to the higher self, more lucid, authentic, and attentive. Giving it this other meaning can stimulate our discernment to choose foods that do not hinder our efforts to reach and maintain a meditative state of mind. A clear example of the sattvic attitude that gives a superior meaning to food is found in the exchange between Yudhiṣṭhira and Bhīṣma, found in the Mahābhāratam:

> *"Yudhiṣṭhira says:*

> *"Tell me clearly, o Knower of Dharma, everything about this subject that comes from dharma itself, about what should be eaten or what should not be eaten, (tell me) all of this. (...)"* 141

> *"Bhīṣma says:*

---

[140] Yoga Sūtra Bhāṣya 3.55
[141] Mahābhāratam 13.116.5

"(...) There is nothing on the Earth that surpasses the taste of meat. For the wounded, the weary, the suffering, for people given to vulgarity, for those given to desire and for those worn out by travel, there is nothing better than meat. It immediately increases vitality and provides the most important part of nutrition. No food is superior to meat, o Destroyer of Enemies.

"However, there are many benefits, o Joy of the Kurus, that come to people that renounce (eating meat). I will describe them. Listen:

"There is no one lower than one who wants to grow their own flesh from the meat of others. This is the cruelest man. Certainly, there is nothing more loved in the world than life itself. This is why one should cultivate compassion for others, as they (hope) for themselves." [142] *(...).*

"(...) We have heard that 'he who feels compassion for others does not fear them.' (...) His fearlessness is a gift from the creatures. Whether injured, unbalanced, fallen, dragged, dejected, all of the creatures protect him, under favorable or unfavorable conditions. Predators don't hurt him, nor do ghosts, nor do demons. He who frees others from fear is liberated in the moment of danger. There has never been and will never be a greater gift than that of life. There is nothing that is more loved by oneself, without a doubt." [143]

"Non-violence is the ultimate dharma. Non-violence is the ultimate control. Non-violence is the ultimate gift. Non-violence is the ultimate penance. Non-violence is the ultimate sacrifice. Non-violence is the ultimate result. Non-violence is the ultimate friend. Non-violence is the ultimate well-being. (...) The non-violent person is like a mother or father to all creatures." [144]

These words of Bhīṣma are taken from a longer dialogue in which he responds to the simple question of whether or not to eat meat. His thought process goes from gross to subtle, starting with the benefits of consuming meat to nourish the body and moving to the ethical arguments in favor of the spiritual benefits of refraining from eating it. This type of reflection that he develops here would also help the mind to find a more sattvic disposition. And, continuing on this same train of thought, we easily arrive at

---

[142] Mahābhāratam 13.116.7 to 12
[143] Mahābhāratam 13.116.23 to 26
[144] Mahābhāratam 13.116.38 to 41.

the conclusion that proper food can lead the mind to the quality of sattvam. Upon reaching the purity of sattvam, the mind becomes a mirror of Paramātmā, which means that food is an important component of the meditation process.

It is not just food that has the power to transform the mind into an instrument better suited to the needs of the meditation. There is a threefold transformation that happens in the mind caused by the act of meditation itself, which we will discuss in the next chapter.

15. Transformations of the Mind

The most popular word used for meditation in Sanskrit is, without a doubt, dhyānam. However, it seems that Patañjali was not very satisfied with the semantic scope of this word, for he brought in two other words that, combined with dhyānam, could more accurately express the idea of 'meditation.' This happens in the third chapter of the Yoga Sūtras, where dhyānam appears as one of the components of *samyama*, the new synonym for meditation. Samyama reinforces dhyānam with two more components: dhāraṇā and samādhi. These three concepts are part of the list of eight components (or limbs) of the method offered by yoga for the practice of meditation. Patañjali defines the concept of meditation as follows:

> *"Dhāraṇā is the fixing of cittam in a certain place. There, (in this place), dhyānam is focus (ekatānatā) on an experience (pratyaya). Samādhi is simply (dhyānam), limited to the mere meaning (of the experience) as if (it were) empty of its own form. The three together are samyama."* [145]

'Dhāraṇā' means, literally, 'support.' Practicing dhāraṇā means bringing the object of attention, whatever it may be, to the conceptual and subjective part of the mind, leaving aside its objective characteristics. Dhāraṇā firmly connects cittam to the space of the heart - the screen on to which Puruṣa projects its meanings. In this way, the mind gains a solid reference base to support its beliefs or opinions, ensuring coherence of its activities with the nature of the higher self. The direct result of the practice of dhāraṇā is the recoiling – *nirodha* – of the activities of the mind to within the inner space (of the heart) as prescribed by Patañjali in sūtra 1.2:

---

[145] Yoga Sūtras 3.1 to 3.4

"Yoga is the recoiling of the activities of cittam." [146]

Dhyānam exercises the ability to fix the inner lens of the mind on a single object, using only the first-person perspective. For dhyānam to be successful, the focus point at both ends of the lens must be adjusted. One focus point needs to be on dhyeyam, the object of meditation, which is actually a subjective image projected on the mental screen. Dhāraṇā has the proper tools to accomplish this task of fixing the attention of cittam on the object of meditation, thus resolving the focus at one end of the lens. At the other end of the scope, the mind engaged in the practice of dhyānam strives to adjust the focus to the attentive gaze of the inner observer (draṣṭā), that is, Puruṣa. The correct adjustment of the lens depends on the mind being protected from disturbances, so that a state of samādhi can be more easily achieved. If this effort is successful, the result of dhyānam will be a mind free of disturbances. Patañjali says:

"The activities of the disturbances should be destroyed by dhyānam" [147]

The effort of dhyānam to free the mind from harm of the disturbances must be able to promote the settling of the cittam (cittaprasādanam). Without the settling of the mind, it is impossible to reach samādhi. Patañjali proposes a little trick to ensure success in this task:

"[The settling of cittam] results from meditation (dhyānam) on that which is pleasant." [148]

Vyāsa comments on this sūtra:

"One should meditate only on that which is pleasant (abhimata). When (the mind) obtains stability there (on that pleasant object), it will also have obtained a position (padam) of stability on other objects." [149]

It is important to understand the meaning of '*meditating on that which is pleasant.*' The object of meditation is pleasant when there is a positive relationship with the vocation of the meditator. A person whose vocation is to work with plants sees a book about botany as a pleasant object. Their dharma evokes meanings originating from Puruṣa that associates concepts such as 'interesting', 'important' and 'pleasant' with the book. For this

---

[146] Yoga Sūtras 1.2
[147] Yoga Sūtras 2.11
[148] Yoga Sūtras 1.39
[149] Yoga Sūtra Bhāṣya 1.39

reason, by placing attention on this pleasant object, the mind is brought closer to the nature of Puruṣa. The result of this closeness is *samādhi*.

Once samādhi is established, the mind surrenders its command over to Īśvara and no longer interferes with cognition. Its aim becomes merely to give comfort and stability to the condition of ekāgratā, through which the meditative focus can remain firmly linked to Puruṣa. This is the condition in which the mind undertakes the task of merely recording in memory the natural meaning attributed by the higher self to the object of meditation. In Sanskrit grammar, the connection between a sign or word and its meaning is called 'yoga' and is only realized in the moments when the mind is operating in conjunction with Puruṣa, that is, when it is in samādhi.

Saṃyama, therefore, resolves the two loose points of the mind's lens, giving it more space, making it more productive, in concrete terms. Over the course of these actions, cittam is transformed and strengthened by the practice of saṃyama, that is, the mind becomes more powerful, both for good and for evil. It is important to remember that in every person's mind, there are many mental nuclei (cittāni); each of them produces vāsanās that try to prevail over the others, alternating the command of antaḥkaraṇam (the internal instrument). But only one of them has the power to stop the mind's impulse towards external activity. Only this one inner mental nucleus does not produce vāsanās (reactive thoughts). Only this one is capable of creating the conditions for recoiling the activities of the mind. It is precisely this inner nucleus that we want to empower with the transformations produced by saṃyama. This is the narrow bridge that leads to the higher self and that redirects the mind's vocation to follow the inspiration of its own dharma.

The two focus points of the cognitive process, one on the observing subject and the other on the observed object, are the two loose ends of dhyānam, resolved by adding dhāraṇā and samādhi to the process of meditation. We will cover the topic of these two focus points in a bit more detail in the next chapter. At the moment, let us better understand the transformative impact of saṃyama on the mind.

Of the eight limbs of the meditation of yoga; dhāraṇā, dhyānam and samādhi are called, collectively, 'the inner limb' by Patañjali. The rest are implicitly qualified as 'external limbs' of the method (sādhanam). Patañjali also claims that the same three limbs are an external limb of 'seedless' yoga (nirbījam). The table below briefly presents this information.

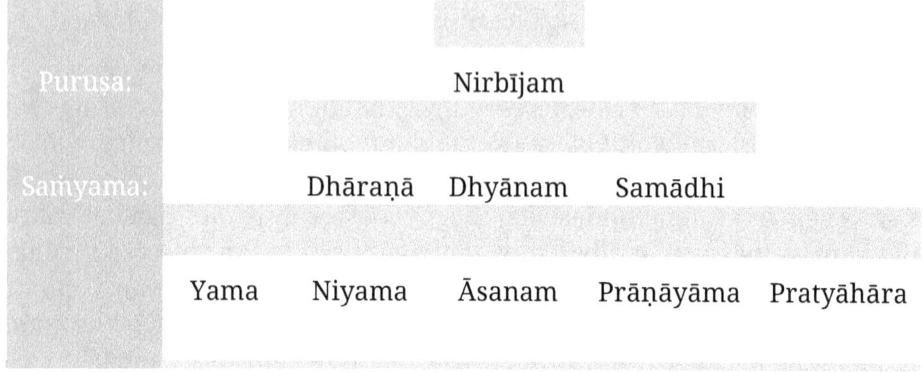

Puruṣa:		Nirbījam		
Saṁyama:		Dhāraṇā	Dhyānam	Samādhi
Yama	Niyama	Āsanam	Prāṇāyāma	Pratyāhāra

Table 4 – Sādhanam in the meditation of yoga.

This table presents the hierarchy that Patañjali found in the process of meditation, proposed by the doctrine of yoga. The bottom row of the table brings together the five 'external' limbs of the sādhanam of meditation. All of these are related to practices that produce noticeable changes in the behavior of the meditator, especially with regard to bodily activities.

The middle line brings together the three 'internal' limbs, or saṁyama, which operate exclusively on the mind, without leaving any perceptible external signs. Patañjali uses the word 'saṁyama' to mean meditation in a greater context, which goes beyond the limitations of 'dhyānam.' The power of meditation (dhyānam) is enhanced by the presence of dhāraṇā and samādhi. Supported by this reinforcement, meditation can produce important transformations in the mind. Saṁyama acts only in the sphere of subjectivity, giving the mind the opportunity to ground itself in its sattvic condition, getting closer to the nature of Puruṣa - whose natural condition is absolute subjectivity.

The top row of the table shows only nirbījam samādhi, which can be considered as a ninth limb of the method, although the system of yoga states that there are only eight. The reason for this discrepancy in numbers is explained by the fact that the method only contemplates practices that use the mind - which is an instrument of Puruṣa. Nirbīja samādhi is produced when the mind, having reached its limit of action, completely withdraws itself from the scene so that Puruṣa alone takes control of the meditation process. Therefore, it is not counted to be one of the limbs of the practice of meditation. Vyāsa describes what happens when the mediator arrives at nirbījam:

"(...) from this point, the mind, having ended its jurisdiction, returns (to its territory) together with the habits conducive to 'isolation' (kaivalyam). In this return (of the mind), Puruṣa rises in the grandeur of its authentic nature, that is, pure, isolated, free. So it is said." [150]

Vyāsa had already explained that there are a variety of samādhis, some of which are of no use to the meditator. Here he distinguishes between only two types. One, called 'sabījam' ('with a seed') by Patañjali, is cultivated through the effort of subtilizing the mind for it to connect to Puruṣa. The other, nirbījam, can only be found by leaving the mind out of the process. The distinction explained by Vyāsa creates an opposition between the two. He says that nirbīja samādhi blocks the intuition of (mental) samādhi and all of the habits produced from intuition. But the fact is that sabīja samādhi is an important part of the natural path that leads the mind to the feet of Puruṣa. The other parts are dhāraṇā and dhyānam - that is, the path is saṁyama.

The path leading to Puruṣa goes through three stages; three transformations (*pariṇāmatrayam*) through which the mind must pass before giving over its command to Puruṣa. Paradoxically, these transformations strengthen the inner nucleus of the mind while also preparing it to relinquish whatever power it has obtained. Patañjali describes these transformations of the mind in the third chapter of the Yoga Sūtras, called 'vibhūti,' meaning, 'power':

"The transformation found through recoiling is the connection of cittam to the moments of recoiling, with the diminishment of habits that lead to dispersion and the emergence of habits that lead to this recoiling. Because of these habits, it flows peacefully." [151]

The first transformation that takes place in cittam is prompted by this *recoiling*. It is considered to be peaceful since it works only on habits, eliminating the automatisms that carry the mind to a state of dispersion. Recognized for stimulating the cultivation of habits that lead the mind to a comfortable recoiling, this transformation favors the arrival and permanence of the mind in the serene condition of samādhi. In the previous chapter, we stated that this recoiling of the mind was related to pratyāhāra, as an externalized version of nirodha. In pratyāhāra, sensory activities of the

---

[150] Yoga Sūtra Bhāṣya 1.51
[151] Yoga Sūtras 3.9 and 3.10

body are brought into the subjective space of the mind. Now, it is these activities of the mind that recoil into the heart - as an offering to the transcendental self, to Paramātmā (or Puruṣa).

Since it results in the strengthening of samādhi, the first transformation of cittam enables the next transformation. Patañjali says:

"Transformation of cittam by samādhi is reached by destroying the multiplicity of meanings and by strengthening the focus (ekāgratā)." [152]

The second transformation of cittam is produced by the sabīja samādhi. Since the mind is stabilized in samādhi, it becomes possible to reach and preserve the condition of ekāgratā, in which it abandons its tendency towards distraction and multiple focus points. Cittam stops searching for different meanings for its object and focusses on a single meaning - ideally, the one that arrives only through the focus point trained directly on Puruṣa.

Vyāsa comments on this second transformation saying that not only the multiplicity of focus points, but also the ability to concentrate on one single focus point are a part of the natural state of the mind. The mind has the natural impulse to feel compelled to follow these two dispositions. This mind is adjusted (to the quality of sattvam, which connects it to Puruṣa) because of its own efforts to destroy and strengthen these two conditions, respectively. This is the transformation of cittam through samādhi.

Patañjali also presents the third transformation of the mind:

"In this case, again, the transformation of cittam by ekāgratā (condition in which there is just one focus point) is the experience of an object in focus (udita), with a backdrop (śāntatulya)." [153]

The third transformation of cittam happens through ekāgratā. The single focus point brings the attention of cittam to only one mental object that stands out and at the same time brings together all other concepts related to that object in a diffuse mass, which starts to form a backdrop. Cittam then concentrates attention on this one object, giving more visibility to the first-person experience (pratyaya). Vyāsa's explanation helps us to better understand this sūtra:

"For the adjusted mind, the previous experience is the backdrop, the

---

[152] Yoga Sūtras 3.11
[153] Yoga Sūtras 3.12

similar and later experiences are what stand out. The mind in samādhi, accompanied by these two experiences, reproduces the same cycle, in the same way, because of its failure to leave samādhi. This, therefore, is the transformation of the mind that receives dharma by ekāgratā. [154]

This description of the third transformation of the mind, already aligned to samādhi, shows that it needs to take one last step when it reaches the state of ekāgratā and gives its attention to an object. Due to the instability of the manifested world, this object will eventually merge with the 'backdrop' and a new object will take the prominent position. To break this cycle, the mind needs to renounce the sabīja samādhi. If it does not detach itself from samādhi, it will be prevented from reaching nirbīja samādhi. This happens because cittam, the mind, belongs to material nature and, as Śaṅkara says in his commentary on the Sūtras:

"The activity of the gunas (material qualities) is movement. As is the activity of the things produced by the gunas. The conditions of these transformations, as a whole, are unstable. An inspiration of unattachment is necessary." [155]

The mind, from the point of view of yoga, is subject to the qualities that characterize the behavior of any material entity. These qualities determine, for example, that entities are permanently subject to transformations. Even the sabīja samādhi of the mind, that connects with Puruṣa, is unstable and impermanent. The threefold transformation of the mind, when it reaches this third stage, triggered again by the changes in the object, returns once more to the beginning - to the recoiling - and enters into a continuous cycle that only ends with an act of unattachment.

The three transformations of the mind produced by saṁyama aim to imprint on the mind and body those characteristics of Puruṣa that can manifest themselves in the material world as meanings attributed to objects. These 'materializable' characteristics of the higher self constitute dharma, and the mind or body that receive these characteristics is called the 'dharmin.' However, the position of the object standing out from or merging with the backdrop has nothing to do with dharma. It has to do with the movement of attention, which jumps to a new object of interest as it moves along with the march of time.

---

[154] Yoga Sūtra Bhāṣya 3.12
[155] Yoga Sūtra Bhāṣya Vivaraṇa 3.12

To close this topic, Patañjali says the following:

"This explains the ways in which the transformations manifest themselves as signs of dharma in the elements and in the organs (that is, in the body). (However), the dharmin (the body that receives the signs of dharma) cannot be described as indistinct (śānta) or distinct (udita) because of its dharma. The difference in development is the cause of the difference in the transformations. From meditation (saṁyama) on the threefold transformation (arises) knowledge of the past and the future." [156]

Saṁyama provides the meditator with the threefold transformation in the mind, making the mind stronger and more focused. The two focus points of attention, the subject and the object, are strengthened in this cyclical process.

We are now able to examine the topic of the two focus points in meditation a little more deeply. And this is precisely what will do in the next chapter.

---

[156] Yoga Sūtras 3.13 and 3.14

16. The Meditative Focus

The phenomenon of cognition depends on the presence of two indispensable elements: a subject who observes and an object that is observed. Each of these occupies its own space (*deśa*), in a location that can be translated by the idea of a focus point. There are two spaces, two opposite focus points, but, when we try to identify a focus point in the cognitive process, we almost always think of the one that points toward the **object**. Rarely does anyone remember the second focus point, the one that points inward, toward the **subject**. The inner focus point should never be overlooked by the meditator. Without it, meditation is not possible.

If the inner focus point is not cared for, the mind ends up moving away from the higher self, seeking meanings indirectly, through knowledge produced by other minds. This can be troublesome if such knowledge, produced by the dharma of others, is not aligned with the dharma of the individual who adopts it. As stated in the Bhagavad Gītā:

"Your dharma carried out poorly is better than the dharma of another well executed. Death in your own dharma is better (because) the dharma of another brings danger." [157]

The 'other,' in the understanding of yoga, does not refer only to another person, as it may seem, but also to other nuclei within the mind of the same person. These nuclei of the mind were briefly described in chapter 13, but it is here in the context of this topic of the focus points where they reveal all of their complexity. Each of them can become the inner focus point of meditation, but only one of these countless nuclei makes a

---

[157] Bhagavad Gītā 3.35

direct connection with Puruṣa possible. Each nucleus functions individually as a complete cittam, capable of producing the five mental activities identified by Patañjali: evidence, inventiveness, imagination, sleep and memory.

Memory is the activity of the mind that best connects an individual to Puruṣa because it ensures Puruṣa a biography and a personality. Anyone who loses their memory, loses their identity. But they do not lose everything. The most important part of memory, produced by the presence of Puruṣa is that which Sanskrit tradition calls *svadharma* - which, fortunately, is not lost, even if the rest of the mind's memory fades. This imperishable, pure memory remains in the mind as a vocation, impulse, or tendency, that is, as dharma imprinted on the objective and subjective bodies. Emanating directly from Puruṣa, it gives meaning to life and shapes thoughts, defining preferences and guiding decisions. Kṛṣṇa, speaking as Puruṣa, states the following:

> *"I am located in the heart of all. Memory, knowledge, and debate come from me. (...)."* [158]

This memory that comes from Puruṣa is already pure, providing an infrastructure for the authentic nature of the meditator. The result of the presence of this dharmic memory is the *adjustment of action* (kriyā yoga). The simplest form of meditation, therefore, consists of only carrying out one's own dharma, that is, 'remembering' Puruṣa. Reminding oneself of the higher self is the best way to place the higher self in the focus point of the subject. Kṛṣṇa says in the Gītā that this meeting with the higher self is not difficult:

> *"For one whose mind is constantly focused, who always remembers me, for this yogi who is always adjusted, I am easy to find."* [159]

Kṛṣṇa speaks placing himself in the role of the higher self of Arjuna. Remembering the higher self means giving the subjective focus of attention over to Puruṣa. In this way, the mind, returning to the condition of a mere instrument, returns Puruṣa to its original role as the subject of the experience. But one should remember that this only works for one single mental nucleus, among the many that vie for control over the inner space of the mind. If this special cittam is not strengthened by the transformations

---

[158] Bhagavad Gītā 15.15
[159] Bhagavad Gītā 8.14

promoted by meditation (saṁyama), the meditator runs the risk of their mind being disturbed by great confusion, with their memories mixing with memories that are not theirs or that are not real. Only the mental nucleus that provides access to Puruṣa can integrate all of the various intelligences and memories into a whole that is coherent with svadharma. Vyāsa comments on this point:

> "If the mind can be apprehended by another mind, by whom is the intelligence of intelligence apprehended? And this one by another and then another. This is the overlap (of intelligences) and confusion of memories. As many memories will be obtained as there are experiences of intelligences of intelligence. And, because of this confusion, there may be uncertainties about each memory. (...). But, Sāṁkhya, yoga and other doctrines agree, in their own words, that Puruṣa is the only lord and enjoyer of the mind." [160]

The following verses from the Bhagavad Gītā deal with this same topic:

> "The man who thinks (of material) objects creates attachment to them. From attachment, desire is created and from desire, anger arises.

> "From anger, illusion arises. From illusion, confusion of memory (arises). From confusion of memory comes loss of intelligence. Once intelligence is lost, (this man) disappears.

> "Conducting oneself with one's senses turned toward objects, but free from desire and aversion, and lead by the higher self (ātmā), one who has submitted themselves to the higher self moves safely towards serenity.

> "From the serenity of this (man) arises the destruction of all suffering. Because of serene awareness, intelligence (buddhi) quickly finds its grounding." [161]

Intelligence (buddhi) and the memory of each one of the innumerable nuclei of the mind should be aligned with the intelligence and memory whose inner focus points to Puruṣa. The only way to remove confusion from the mind is to convince it to surrender its vision to Puruṣa so as to ensure that only Puruṣa's own meanings are evoked. The correct way to ensure the presence of Puruṣa be in the focus point of the subject is called

---

[160] Yoga Sūtra Bhāṣya 4.21
[161] Bhagavad Gītā 2.62 to 2.65

Kriyā Yoga - adjustment of action, by Patañjali. Formed by three of the niyamas, Kriyā Yoga is presented right at the beginning of the second chapter of the Yoga Sūtras and is detailed a bit further on in the same chapter:

"The alignment of action is purification (tapas), self-observation (svādhyāya) and surrender to Īśvara (Īśvarapraṇidhānam). Its purpose is to produce samādhi and minimize disturbances." [162]

"From the destruction of impurities through purification arises the perfection of all bodily senses. From self-observation comes integration with the deity of your choice (Iṣṭā Devatā). From surrender to Īśvara comes the perfection of samādhi." [163]

The three components of aligning actions affect the meditative focus of cognition. Purification promoted by *tapas* removes from this inner focus the presence of that which is not aligned with one's personal dharma. In this way, cognition gains a certain capacity for critical thinking, becoming more transparent - as if all of the bodily senses were working close to perfectly. The second component of Kriyā Yoga, *svādhyāya*, acts on self-awareness, facilitating the choice of a sensory channel (*devatā*) that will serve as the path to integrate the mind with Īśvara. The origin of the word 'svādhyāya' is the verb 'adhī', which means 'to observe,' 'to be aware.' It should be noted that the word 'devatā' (deity) allows for a religious understanding, of a devotional nature, but it also allows for a philosophical understanding, in which each of the five senses are identified. In fact, when Ādi Śaṁkarācārya elaborates the Smarta doctrine for the Hindu Dharma, he contemplates exactly five 'iṣṭadevatās' - even the number coincides: Gaṇeśa, Viṣṇu, Śakti, Śiva and Sūrya.

The third and final component of Kriyā Yoga *Īśvara praṇidhānam* corresponds exactly with the surrender of the inner focus of attention to Puruṣa, producing samādhi as a result. For this reason, this component also appears in the first chapter of the Yoga Sūtras[164], which deals specifically with samādhi, in the passage in which Īśvara is described as one of the aspects assumed by Puruṣa.

There is reason to believe that this formula presented by Patañjali to resolve the fixing of the inner meditative focus point is not original. The

---

[162] Yoga Sūtras 2.1 and 2.2
[163] Yoga Sūtras 2.43 to 2.45
[164] Yoga Sūtras 1.23

proposal of adjusting one's actions permeates the entire Bhagavad Gītā, where proper action (adjusted to the higher self) is called 'niyataṁ karma' - behavior that that leads to the realization of svadharma. Note that the word 'niyata', 'recoiled inward' is very close to 'niyama', 'inner control.' Both are derived from the verb 'ni-yam', 'withhold within.' Adjustment of action in the Gītā is called Karma Yoga:

"One who, having subdued the organs of action with the mind, sits with the deluded spirit (vimūḍha) evoking memory of the objects of the senses, they are called fake.

"But one who, having subdued the organs of action with the mind, o Arjuna, begins to practice with the organs of action the adjustment of their acts (karmayoga), unattached, they stand out.

"Carry out the proper action yourself (niyataṁ karma) - action is in fact superior to non-action (omission). You would not even be able to complete your bodily journey if you give yourself over to inaction." [165]

"It is better to (follow) your own dharma, (even if) badly than to perfectly follow another's. By carrying out actions aligned with your own nature, you do not incur sin." [166]

Niyataṁ karma is action inspired by svadharma, which becomes possible only when the focus point of the subject is trained on the higher self, Puruṣa. According to the teachings of yoga, when we allow the mind to settle quietly in the center of the inner space, protected from external interferences, we can ensure the presence of the higher self as the focus of the subject. The settled mind easily finds its source of dharma, that is, that one mental inner nucleus endowed with the capacity to produce the recoiling of mental activities. It is the only *cittam* that gives meaning to the meditator's life. It frees the individual from their desires, for it reveals that they already have everything they could want, for svadharma is the very structure that gives shape and support to their inner space.

The adjustment of action, according to the Gītā, depends on the adjustment of memory, for the meditator is unable to evoke in their memory objects of the senses. According to Sanskrit tradition, memory can be built in two ways, which complement each other: disturbed and undisturbed. Disturbed memory is memory that receives interference from external events

---

[165] Bhagavad Gītā 3.6 to 3.8
[166] Bhagavad Gītā 18.47

and objects, and is objective in nature, equivalent to a third-person account. Undisturbed memory, on the other hand, is non-localized and develops subjectively, independent of any other phenomena external to the person who enjoys it. It does not refer to objects, but only to the subject. It can only be expressed by poetic images whose meanings are in the first-person, and which refer directly to the mythical foundations of the mind. Patañjali places memory among the five basic activities of the mind and its importance begins to reveal itself when it is listed as one of the three tools that allow for the meditator to capture their intuition:

"The [saṁprajñāta] of others originates in an intuition of samādhi retained by memory, by strong will and by faith." [167]

The term 'saṁprajñāta' is used by Patañjali to identify an intuition (prajñā) produced only by samādhi when it reaches consciousness. This intuitive experience, when perceived, is useful to the meditator as an indicator of intensity or proximity to samādhi. The importance of memory to capture saṁprajñāta is confirmed by Vyāsa's comment:

"The experience of this method is (appropriate) for yogis. Faith is the settling of the mind (cetas). Like a kind mother, it protects the yogi. Certainly, a firm disposition arises for the faithful seeker of discernment. Memory is fixed with the one in whom the firm disposition arose. And, with the fixation of memory, the mind is free from confusion and is placed in samādhi. For the mind in samādhi, discernment of intuition arises, whereby the object (vastu) is perceived as meaning. From continuous practice (of this method) and of the unattachment from the object (viṣaya), non-saṁprajñāta samādhi (arises)." [168]

As memory can exist as disturbed or undisturbed, we can see here that Vyāsa is referring to undisturbed memory (akliṣṭa). This means memory with wisdom, that is, purified memory. Regarding this topic, Patañjali says:

"In the purification of memory, 'thoughts devoid of bodily experience' (nirvitarka), are as if emptied of their own form, limited to the mere meaning (of the experience). In this way, both reflection and (thought) devoid of reflection are also explained in the subtle sphere. The degree of subtlety rises to the 'aliṅgam' condition." [169]

---

[167] Yoga Sūtras 1.20
[168] Yoga Sūtra Bhāṣya 1.20
[169] Yoga Sūtras 1.43 to 1.45

Memory is the most subjective of the five mental activities that Patañjali refers to in his Sūtras. When he refers to purification of memory, he gives memory the status of an escape from the material universe, as its degree of subtlety extends to the 'aliṅgam' ('one who has no distinguishing marks'). This is precisely the condition in which the non-manifested pradhānam is found, as original undifferentiated matter. Purification of memory, therefore, can give a strong boost to the purification of the mind, making it more sattvic and prone to finding Puruṣa within the process of meditation. To make this importance of memory even clearer, Patañjali repeats the same words used in the sutras cited above, in his brief definition of samādhi:

"Samādhi is just this, (dhyānam), limited to the mere meaning (of the experience) as if (it were) empty of its own form." [170]

The mind here produces meditative thinking, dhyānam, and the purification of memory is implied, because without it, mediative thinking can not be sustained. Purification of memory is the act of removing the past from the role of foundation for the present. In purified memory, factual information of the past no longer exists, and the only thing that can be extracted from it are meanings of a subtle nature converted into myths that are adjusted only by narrative time, eternally present. Unattachment to past events purifies memories, and, in the process, leads to a cultivated samādhi, that which is called 'sabījam', that is, 'seeded.' Unattachment from past events prepares the meditator for the unexpected and gives them the inspiration they need, at any time, to start their story over.

When actions are aligned, the information memorized about them becomes 'mythologized', that is, they are purified, becoming mythical narratives - typically expressions of inhales and exhales of Puruṣa. Through these, the meditator can learn and narrate their own story as if in an epic, which Sanskrit culture regards as the true story of life. Just as the mythologization of the body makes the material organism into a miniature of the universe, in which all the characters of the mythical narratives live and act, this also happens with actions when they are aligned with dharma. They too are converted into micro-universes. Vyāsa leaves no doubt about this in his commentary on svādhyāya ('self-observation'):

"The devas, the ṛṣis and the siddhas become visible to one who

---

habitually practices self-observation. And resides in that person's work." [171]

The meditative state is one in which the mind remains balanced and neutral, supported by the two focus points of meditation. It is relatively easy to maintain focus on the object, as small variations in the focus of attention are normal and happen all the time. They help, generally, to build a clearer idea about the object of perception. The difficult thing is to regain the meditative focus, because when it is lost, discernment and intuition are lost along with it. The 'adjustment of action' (Karma or Kriyā Yoga) circumvents this difficulty and organizes the mind, placing Puruṣa in the focus point of the **subject** of the mind. As such, what remains is to regulate the attention that the mind places on the meditation process, in order to consolidate the control gained over actions. After all, the Gītā says:

"(...)Therefore, adjust yourself to yoga. Yoga is excellence in actions." [172]

17. Fine-tuning Attention

Your attention is a very valuable asset; and not just for you, as a precious natural gift, but in terms of actual economic value, market value even. Perhaps when thinking about this on a small, individual scale, it may be challenging to put a price on your attention, however, if you do the math to calculate how much the market, industry, politicians, service providers, etc. pay for your attention; you may notice something different. We simply

---

[171] Yoga Sūtra Bhāṣya 2.44
[172] Bhagavad Gītā 2.50

need to take a look at the huge amount of money spent daily on advertising accounts to realize the importance attention holds in the economic world. Perhaps, then, the fact that people's attention is indeed the only force in this world that can move the gears of the economy will not come as such a surprise. The first commandment for those seeking success in business is to know where the market's attention is going at any given moment. And the second commandment is to adjust to this force so that the business will always be in favor of the interests of the market.

Returning to the area of meditation, attention also has an important role to play here in the economy of meanings that move the currency of the mind. The difference is that the gratification for the effort made in the pursuit of success on sustaining attention does not come in the form of material goods, but in the form of happiness (*ānanda*). Happiness will be the topic of the next chapter. For now, it is important to reflect a bit more on this topic of attention - which can be responsible for both happiness and for the ruin of a life.

The most used Sanskrit terms for 'attention' come from the verb *dhā*, which means 'to place' (in this case, 'place the mind'): *praṇidhānam*; *avadhānam* or *avadhi*; and *samādhānam* or *samādhi*. These terms, however, are not exactly synonymous with each other. The word *praṇidhānam* – used by Patañjali in the expression *Īśvarapraṇidhānam'* (*'surrendering to Īśvara'*) - refers to attention that is turned inward, strongly linked to the focus point of the subject. The word *avadhānam* expresses the more common concept of attention, which focusses primarily on the object perceived by the mind. But the type of attention that is of interest to the yogi is *samādhi*, attention that is not dependent on the mind, but simply connects the two opposite focus points to which the mind points, the focus on the object and the focus on the subject. In this case, the mind's role is exclusively to ensure that perception is pure, isolated from any external or internal interference, firmly anchored in the present. In order to reach this state of attention corresponding to the samādhi of yoga, the mind needs to eliminate from its inner space any memories, habits or desires that may feed any kind of dependance on the external world.

The mind sometimes behaves like a child at play, driven by curiosity from here to there. Curiosity (*kutūhalam*) results from desire and produces unreliable attention because it creates agitation in the mind. Attention created by curiosity, by the mere desire to know, is not even a subject discussed in meditation literature. Like a child, the bouncy and curious mind needs to be gently guided to a condition of tranquility, in which it can find its authentic nature, its vocation, and adopt this as reference for its behavior. Like a child, the mind needs to be educated, or re-educated, so that it can become a useful instrument for the higher self. The education of the mind is, essentially, education of attention.

Attention is the mind's ability to guide the representative image of a particular object into Puruṣa's line of sight, or gaze, keeping this image there for as long as necessary for Puruṣa to attribute spontaneous meaning to the object. The intensity of attention can be measured by the time over which the mind is able to maintain the visible representation (*dṛśyam*) of the object available to the gaze (*dṛśi*) of the higher self. Or it can be measured by the clarity of the meaning obtained for the object. The maximum intensity of attention is only obtained when the mind finds a meditative state.

When the mind is in a meditative state, it is in a state of internal coherence in which dhāraṇā fixes the mind on the inner space in a sustainable way, dhyānam produces a flow of cognition that allows for an experience to be constructed and the intense, steady and comforting attention of samādhi produces happiness (*ānanda*). The key to achieving and maintaining a meditative state is to connect oneself only to the meaning of the object and not to the object itself, which ceases to exist for the mind. To connect with meaning is to find personal and subjective understanding of the object of cognition. When the higher self illuminates an object with the light of understanding, attention stabilizes naturally and sustainably.

Gaining control over attention is a priority that needs to be resolved by the meditator. The inattentive mind, even if it is fully conscious, is unable to settle itself and deliver its information to Puruṣa. As a result, meanings stop being attributed to information and the understanding needed for the information to become useful does not develop. The result of the lack of understanding is confusion. Understanding only exists in Puruṣa and confusion, only in manas. Sāṁkhya Kārikā uses the expression 'instability in manas'(*'mano'navasthānam'*) to designate the condition of the inattentive mind. Attention has a lot to do with the two focus points of the mind, but the key point is understanding. Gauḍapāda's commentary on this expression states:

"One who whose mind (cittam) is unfocussed (vyagra) does not

understand, even if the story is very well told." [173]

The instability in *manas* leaves *cittam* unfocused and without understanding, because the role of manas is to make a stable connection of cittam with each of the two focus points of cognition. Stability is achieved when the information processing cycle of the mind follows the breathing cycle of Puruṣa. The inhalation (*apāna*) is the movement produced by *ahaṁkāra* that walks toward the higher self, carrying inward the information that will be offered to the gaze of Puruṣa. The inner pause (*antaḥkumbhakam*) is the moment when the mind must annul itself and allow for Puruṣa's enjoyment. Finally, the exhalation (*prāṇa*) is the movement produced by *buddhi* that emanates from Puruṣa bringing meaning and understanding of the object to the mind.

Understanding is the visible face of Puruṣa within each individual. They are the light that reveals to the mind the path of transcendence, which goes beyond the limits of this world. Understanding is called by many names in Sanskrit, such as *avadhāraṇa* ('certainty'), *cetanā* ('consciousness'), *avabodha* ('clear perception'), *avagama* ('comprehension'), *pratibhā* ('light'); all of these relate to the idea of clarity that comes from above, in this case, directly from Puruṣa.

Kṛṣṇa says, referring to Puruṣa:

"They are also the light of lights. They are said to be beyond darkness. They are knowledge that should be known, present in each person's heart, accessible through knowledge." [174]

The mind's receptivity to the meanings attributed by Puruṣa can be enhanced by strengthening attention. Attention can be passive or active. In both cases, it indicates the intensity with which the two focus points of consciousness are connected. Passive attention is inadequate for meditation as it weakens the presence of Puruṣa in the focus point of the subject. It arises when the mind is carried away by desire caused by external interferences, postponing or refusing the commands of Puruṣa. In summary, passive attention leads the mind to be guided by improper intuitions. Active attention works with intentionality, *saṁkalpa* because it is the result of the deliberate will of the individual. The commands of Īśvara arise in the mind as adjusted intelligence, *yukta-buddhi,* as a series of understandings that

---

[173] Sāṁkhya Kārikā Bhāṣya 7
[174] Bhagavad Gītā 13.18

manas can capture and adopt in order to illuminate one's thoughts or narratives. Vyāsa says, in the Mahābhāratam:

> *"Manas should make a lamp (pradīpa) with the senses that best represent intelligence (buddhi), as is done similarly in meditation by those who cultivate indifference (to the things of the world)."* [175]

In this verse, it is clear that Vyāsa is speaking of the intelligence that comes from Puruṣa, pertaining to the sattvam condition of the mind. The light of true understanding is only lit in the mind that has achieved the purity of the sattvam condition. But how does one know if the mind has reached the condition of sattvam? It is Kṛṣṇa who responds in the Gītā:

> *"When there arises light and knowledge in every door of this body, then one can know that sattvam is abundant."* [176]

In the above verse, 'light' means understanding that only exists if the meditator regularly cultivates active attention. The light of understanding also appears only in the sattvic mind, whose purity makes it a witness to the presence of Puruṣa. Apparently, the exercise of attention and the sattvic purity of the mind, both producers of understanding, have some sort of connection with one another. This is precisely what the sage Vasiṣṭha says to the prince Rāma:

> *"The true appearance (of the world) arises from the purified mind, just like (the true appearance) of a jewel when its dirt is rubbed away. From continued practice in holding steady (attention) on one (focus point) for a long time, comes purification of the mind (cetas). Free from the trampling of intentions, the light of understanding (pratibhā) appears in the mind."* [177]

According to what Vasiṣṭha said, continually exercising attention, strengthening it, results in the purification of the mind. But active attention must be cultivated, for if Puruṣa's gaze is not present, the tools of the mind or body will not be sufficient to attribute any meaning to the object. It will be a lost gaze in which the mind is only wandering without finding any understanding of the object that it would like to give its attention to.

Vasiṣṭha also offered another important tip, when stating that the

---

[175] Mahābhāratam 12.248.12
[176] Bhagavad Gītā 14.11
[177] Yoga Vāsiṣṭha 4.17.20 and 4.17.21

purified mind is free from being overrun by intentions (saṁkalpas) which are elements that attract our attention to desires that populate the mind. To a certain extent, attention is responsible for creating attachment, as desire is not able to be expressed without attention being passively mobilized. That which does not awaken the force of attention never actually exists in our subjective space. If the mind is free from intentions that are not adjusted to its dharma, this means it is functioning in tune with the one inner nucleus capable of connecting to Puruṣa.

Aside from this cittam that communicates with the higher self, no other mental inner nucleus of antaḥkaraṇam is able to reach and maintain the condition of sattvam in the mind. When this one cittam reaches the state of sattvam in a sustainable way, it becomes a leader for the other nuclei and ends up being spontaneously imitated by any other impersonal 'self' that exists within the mind. Hence, Puruṣa's qualification as the 'enjoyer' within the body is understood.

> *"In this body, the supreme Puruṣa is called the beholder (Upadraṣṭā), he who authorizes, who sustains, enjoys, is the great sovereign (Maheśvara) and supreme higher self (Paramātmā)."* [178]

Puruṣa is, in fact, the only enjoyer of all experiences of the body or mind. It is reasonable to believe, taking into consideration Sanskrit culture, that Puruṣa is actually the only source of consciousness and of attention. Access to these resources of subjective life is directly proportional to the purity of the mind that attains the sattvam quality, by which it becomes full of understanding and becomes illuminated. All the brilliance of the sattvam mind has its root in the center of the first-person universe and without it, Puruṣa would be incapable of seeing this world at all.

To summarize: attention is important in meditation because it directs the two great movements of breath of Puruṣa. Based on the mental image of the object, the inhalation carries information through ahaṁkāra directly to Puruṣa. From Puruṣa, the exhale carries meaning through buddhi directly to the mental inner nucleus to which attention is linked. The result of attention is a personal experience and, with it, the happiness resulting from understanding. This works well, as long as the focus points are adjusted to the true nature of the meditator and not to their desires or aversions. This is the only way that attention can capture the subject

---

[178] Bhagavad Gītā 13.23

impartially so that it can be observed correctly by the higher self. This is dhyānam for Patañjali.

Attention that is reeducated and adjusted to the higher self gives us, as a reward for our effort, a priceless asset: immortality; that is, a full and happy existence with the mind identified with Puruṣa.

18. The Happy Mind

In the cultural universe of the Sanskrit language, one of the expected results from the correct practice of meditation is a state of well-being in the body and mind, accompanied by a gentle and pleasant sensation of bliss: *ānanda*. In the context of meditation, this feeling can be translated as a profound spiritual happiness, indicative of succeeding in the task of connecting the mind to Puruṣa. In the modern history of yoga, great teachers carry the word ānanda in their spiritual names: Vivekānanda (*'the happiness of discernment'*), Yogānanda (*'the happiness of yoga'*), Śivānanda (*'the happiness of Śiva'*), Kuvalayānanda (*'the happiness of the blue lotus'*). Much importance is given to this feeling by meditators in the Hindu tradition.

Happiness is the feeling that affects an individual in response to the benign meaning attributed by the individual themselves to some situation or object of attention. This meaning has the power to give that situation or object a comforting, pleasant or pleasurable appearance. The result is the relaxation of the body, a spontaneous smile, lightness of the mind and the conviction that everything is going well. The feeling of happiness manifests itself as a result of any situation to which the mind attributes that benign meaning, even if it is not true.

In order to achieve ānanda, true happiness, we must take care in opening the eyes of the mind to assign a true meaning to all situations, objects and people that appear in the objective focus point of our consciousness. This meaning is always subjective, from the first-person perspective, and can be misguided if the meditator is removed from the subjective focus point – such as when one might be experiencing low self-esteem and seek social acceptance by copying collective behavior patterns. But if meditation is practiced correctly, without interference of hidden desires, it is a quick and sure way to reach ānanda.

It is quick, but it is not easy. A part of modern literature has portrayed meditation as if it were a process that can be switched on for some time and then switched off after, to return to our normal routine. Not much is said about the permanent and stable meditative state that can be reached, without needing to turn it on or off, but only to replenish it. Apparently, the meditative state is not thought of these days as a way for the mind to find a stable and fluid satisfying attitude. It is rare to find authors such as Daniel Goleman, who, when referring to the mental state of being in 'flow' in his book 'Emotional Intelligence' describes something similar to the meditative state, although using the metaphor of an athletic track:

> *"Athletes know this state of grace as 'the zone,' where excellence becomes effortless, crowd and competitors disappearing into a blissful, steady absorption in the moment."* [179]

On the other hand, in Sanskrit literature, there are plenty of examples of expressions that are used to unequivocally describe a serene and long-lasting meditative state:

> *"It is said that a sthitadhīmuni (sage with a settled mind) is one who has no more desires, fears or anger."* [180]

> *"Devoid of desires, yatacittātmā ('with cittam controlled by the higher self'), with all ambition abandoned..."* [181]

> *"yuktena manasā ('with an adjusted mind') we are in the drive given by the god Savitā, with the strength to reach heaven."* [182]

> *"The samāhita ('one who has a calm and attentive mind') should look at a subtle mark with unmoving eyes..."* [183]

All these terms define a mind adjusted to dharma, pointing towards a sustainable state of attention that can be achieved by any creature. The mind, when it is not agitated, spontaneously gravitates towards a meditative state, because it produces stability and comfort that promote

---

[179] Goleman, Daniel. Emotional Intelligence: Why It Can Matter More Than IQ (p. 90). Random House Publishing Group. Kindle edition.
[180] Bhagavad Gītā 2.56
[181] Bhagavad Gītā 4.21
[182] Śvetāśvatara Upaniṣad 2.2
[183] Haṭha Yoga Pradīpikā 2.31

relaxation and make it much happier and more productive.

As such, with so many rewards at the end of the line, it should be easy for the mind to find the energy to seek this state intentionally, but it is rebellious and resists. Therefore, a great effort must be made to control the mind until it can be convinced to relax and enjoy the well-being resulting from loosening its inner tethers. To lessen this difficulty, a path needs to be found that leads the mind naturally to a meditative state.

Humans are probably the only species on the planet capable of surviving with the mind outside of a meditative state. This anomaly may be the consequence of an evolutionary advantage: the ability to give intentional, non-spontaneous meaning to information that is brought in by sensory pathways. Human beings may have developed the capacity to change the meaning of this information more than any other species. And this allows humans to create and share culture (*dharma*), providing all of the tools needed to express the richness of one's inner, subjective life in a personal way. All the wonder of being human is due to the conscious and intentional sharing, through language, of a dharma created by one's own ingenuity. A part of the transformations (or *pariṇāma*) that affect human evolution are due to cultural exchange, to the exchange of meanings. And this is the same as moving Puruṣa away from the focus point of the subject of cognition.

The human capacity to survive with the higher self removed from the meditative focus point brings with it another, much darker, side: it gives the mind the power to lie, not to mimic and survive, but to steal other meanings and pretend to think what it does not actually think. Accepting one's own lie deceives the mind, dulling discernment and making the mind believe the lies of others, becoming easy prey to the evil of others.

To escape this trap, the meditator should seek the truth to build over it the foundation of their own personal culture (*svadharma*). This is the good side of the human ability to attribute intentional meaning: when there is commitment to the truth, a meditative state can be achieved by one's own merit. It is not nature that imposes a meditative state on the mind. It is meditation itself, practiced voluntarily, that enables the meditator to find their own authentic nature. And this is how one finds much more than just their place in the order of the universe: one finds happiness.

Bliss, as we might call the meditator's happiness, is called ānanda, in Sanskrit. And we all know that the mind is always searching for happiness. Let us now try to discover why that is, starting with a reference provided by one of the tantric yogic texts:

"Unique, ineffable happiness, growing in the heart of the yogīśvaras who enjoy samādhi attentive to nāda, the only one who experiences this is the Lord Guru Nātha." [184]

This is not about worldly happiness, as Śrī Guru Nātha is just another name for Śiva ('the benign one'), that higher self that resides in the heart of all creatures. In the Upaniṣads, he is usually called Brahma, the inner higher self:

"The inner higher self (antarātmā) is a person (puruṣa) the size of a thumb, permanently seated in the heart of mortals, connected with the reflective mind of the heart. Those who know this become immortal." [185]

Ānanda is a feeling that invades the mind when it feels the presence of the inner higher self (Brahma). It can be adopted by the meditator as a reliable indicator of the success of their practices. Surely, this is one of the reasons why so many yogis adopt ānanda as part of their spiritual name. And it is not only in the names of the yogis that this word appears with some prominence. Let us continue to understand a little more about the nuances of its many meanings.

The popularity of Vedānta in the west made the expression 'saccidānanda' very well known, formed by the union of three words: *sat* ('existence'), *cit* ('consciousness') and *ānanda* ('happiness'). There are two distinct meanings for this expression, the first of which was adopted by instructors connected with Vedānta. According to their interpretation, the three words define the three main attributes of Brahma. With this interpretation, the same weight and same category are given to each of the three words, which come together on equal ground to say that the attributes of Brahma are *'existence, consciousness and happiness.'*

But there is a second understanding, one found in Vedic literature, that seems to fit better with the tradition of yoga. According to this one, the three words have differing weights, and greater emphasis is given to the word ānanda, to which the other two become adjectives. In the Tejobindu Upaniṣad, we find a good reference to illustrate this second interpretation. In the third chapter, a conversation is described between Śiva and his son Kumāra, who asks:

---

[184] Haṭha Yoga Pradīpikā 4.81
[185] Śvetāśvatara upaniṣad 3.13

"Tell me about the experience of the higher self." [186]

Kumāra wants to know how Śiva, who is the higher self, lives his own existence in the world. Śiva responds to his son with a series of short phrases, of which we highlight the following two:

"I am the form of supreme happiness (parānanda) of existence (sat). I am the form of supreme happiness of consciousness (cit)." [187]

And finally, Śiva concludes:

I am the eternal, awakened, pure, only happiness of existence and of consciousness (saccidānanda)." [188]

These passages were written in a way that seems to suggest that *sat* and *cit* hold the position of adjectives, that they function as qualifiers of *ānanda*. In this text, *happiness* (ānanda) is the way in which *existence* (sat) and *consciousness* (cit) are experienced by the meditator. Sat and cit can be considered to be more than mere attributes of Brahma. They are synonymous of Brahma. This means that the expression saccidānanda is a perfect equivalent to brahmānanda - the happiness of Brahma.

Brahmānanda is the name of the second part of the Taittirīya Upaniṣad, which discusses the search for the true higher self among the various selves that live within us. First it speaks of annamayātmā, the higher self of the body, made of food. Next, it speaks of prāṇamayātmā, the higher self made of movement. It also speaks of the higher self made of reason, manomayātmā, and then of the higher self made of knowledge, vijñānamayātmā. And finally, it speaks of ānandamayātmā - the higher self made of happiness, whereby the meditator reaches their goal.

Through ānandamayātmā, seeking the happiness of brahma, the meditator abandons fear (of being oneself) and reaches the true higher self, far from any kind of oppression and away from any duality of the mind. This is the meaning of saccidānanda in the Upaniṣads - happiness (bliss) that leads to true consciousness, arising from the self that inhabits our hearts and can be reached only through meditation.

When the happiness of Brahma is manifested, it is manifested as one of the saṁprajñātas (indicators of the presence of samādhi) mentioned by

---

[186] Tejobindu Upaniṣad 3.1
[187] Tejobindu Upaniṣad 3.8
[188] Tejobindu Upaniṣad 3.11

Patañjali in the sūtra that says:

"Samprajñāta takes shape from vitarka, vicāra, ānanda and asmitā." [189]

Vyāsa's commentary on this sūtra makes it clear that happiness is one of the possible ways to experience samādhi:

"vitarka is the experience (ābhoga, enjoyment) of the mind in the physical (the body), vicāra is the subtle (experience), ānanda is joy, asmitā is 'unified consciousness' (ekātmikā saṁvid). Of these, the first of the list is samādhi with bodily experience (savitarka), the second is devoid of bodily experience (but) with subjective (subtle) experience, the third is devoid of subjective experience but with happiness, the fourth is devoid of the 'other' (tad vikala), it is pure selfness (asmitāmātra). These are all of the samādhis with support." [190]

This means that to feel ānanda indicates to the meditator that they are close to the correct samādhi, the one which Vyāsa says is correct for the development of yoga. Happiness, in addition to signaling the presence of samādhi in the mind, makes the path to meditating much more pleasant. And, most importantly, there is the possibility that the mind be led to samādhi following the reverse path, starting from a state of true happiness. Therefore, one must discover how to produce ānanda.

Ānanda is not ordinary third-person happiness, produced by external causes. Ānanda is existential happiness experienced in the first-person, which arises spontaneously whenever there is the feeling that everything is exactly as it should be. It is the happiness of living authentically, doing what you love, in your own way, with freedom. When one is overcome by a feeling of gratitude, even without knowing who or what to thank, the mind is flooded by the force of happiness.

Ānanda is the feeling that is also felt when we enjoy or create art - the most democratic doorway to happiness. Art is the exercise of the freest expression of the higher self; this is why it is able to mobilize liberating mental forces. It is why art is thought to be therapeutic in nature, capable of raising self-esteem and strengthening the artist's sense of independence and nonconformity. Puruṣa experiences happiness each time they are able to see their own expression echoed in the activities of the mind. Art is the language of Puruṣa - the pure flow of feeling and spontaneous signification

---

[189] Yoga Sūtras 1.17
[190] Yoga Sūtra Bhāṣya 1.17

- a language that speaks for itself without allowing for any translation.

Enjoying art makes the mind happy. Happiness makes the mind more transparent and more attuned to the heart, resulting in wisdom. The wise mind removes from its inner space all obstacles to the expression of Puruṣa, becoming more focused and gaining more spiritual depth.

19. Time in Meditation

There are two common ways of approaching the question of time in meditation. The first one looks at time in a very simple way, as a measure of the extent of meditation. The other way of studying time in meditation sees it as part of the mechanism of perception, as an indispensable component in the process of capturing information. Sensory perception of the objective world only takes place when the organs of perception capture successive changes of appearance, state or movement of the object. Understood in this second way, time becomes an important condition for the manifestation of consciousness.

The ideal duration of meditation is as long as it takes for Puruṣa's presence to be revealed in the mind. It does not matter to the meditator whether the meditation lasts only a fraction of a second or an eternity. If the meditation is correct, time doesn't count. Meditation does not need to be measured by the length of its duration but by the depth it reaches or by the attention it garners. The ideal length of meditation is the time that attention can be comfortably sustained on the object of meditation.

However, the length of a meditation sometimes impresses even experienced researchers. Daniel Goleman and Richard Davidson use the expression *'Olympic-level meditators'* [191] to describe people who meditate six hours a day or more. This assessment, however, doesn't make much sense as meditation cannot be evaluated only by its duration. The quality of the meditative state and the inner happiness that is achieved must also be included in this calculation. When a meditation is performed with an

---

[191] Goleman, Daniel. The Science of Meditation: How to Change Your Brain, Mind and Body (p. 4). Penguin Books Ltd. Kindle edition.

'adjusted mind' (*yuktena manasā*), it can comfortably last forever.

Time is portrayed in Sanskrit literature in a slightly richer way, as a mythical entity. Time, in Sanskrit, is called kāla, whose origin is usually traced to the homonymous noun kāla ('black') which relates to the destruction by fire of the god Rudra. Its etymology, however, shows that kāla is a word derived from the root verb 'kal', which means to 'calculate.' In fact, we should note the relationship between time and the astrological calculations used to determine propitious or unfavorable moments to manifest the *puruṣārthas* - (meanings of Puruṣa).

Sanskrit culture holds great respect for astrology; whose tools make it possible to determine the *janmakāla*, the exact moment of birth, when dharma is impressed on the body, and becomes active for that individual. Astrology also identifies a series of eventualities that unfold throughout our lives (*Āyus*) offering a series of favorable occasions for the expression of Puruṣa. And the scope of these calculations ends at the unpredictability of the moment of death (*antakāla*, or *mṛtyukāla*), which closes the long sequence of opportunities for learning and practicing *svarūpam*, the embodied dharma of the meditator.

The relationship of time with the length of life and with individual dharma is further revealed by the fact that the god Yama, who governs death, is also called Dharma or Dharmarāja. Duration and subjection to dharma are typical characteristics of material nature; from which we can conclude that time only affects material qualities, having no effect on Puruṣa. The Kaṭha Upaniṣad 1.2.8 says, referring to ātmā:

"(The higher self) is not born nor do they die. This sage does not originate or become anything. This unborn, eternal, constant, primordial is not killed when the body dies."

Note that the higher self is defined in this verse by denying its temporality. If meditation is an exercise of the higher self, which is not touched by time, practiced by the mind, which is subject to the transformations of time, how can time become yet another tool for the meditator? The mind needs change, needs objects in motion and transformation; without these things it is unable to perceive the present. But the higher self (Puruṣa) does not change. They are in the immutable first-person universe, out of reach of the activities of the mind. How does time contribute to the integration of the mind with Puruṣa in the context of meditation?

When the mind wants to perceive Puruṣa, it focuses on things that transform, seeking in them only the meaning of transformation and not the object that is transformed. The mind searches for signs of Puruṣa by placing its attention on the meaning of the transformation and thus immerses itself in narrative time, the mind itself being captured by a narrative. From the depths of this narrative time, from the 'once upon a time...,' meanings of mythical nature arise, indicating the presence of Puruṣa. In mythical time, there is no past nor future, but only the present eternalized by the flow of the narrative, which puts the mind in the position of virtual witness of the narrated events. Mythical narratives have the magical power of making the mind indifferent to time.

Indifference to time leads the mind to focus on the present moment, strengthening its bond with the higher self. Being aware of opportunities for transformation or action adjusted to one's own nature makes the light of Īśvara illuminate the mind through its dharma, without creating the need for the mind to abandon its connection with the past or future. It is enough to be in tune with one's dharma and purge false memories so that benign thoughts may populate the educated mind of the meditator.

Throughout the fourth chapter of the Yoga Sūtras, Patañjali teaches us that, in the uneducated mind, memories determine the past and habits determine the future. Common thoughts (vāsanās), which result from memories and habits, follow one another in the mind, produced by the path they follow, continuously linking the past and the future. Although they are natural, these internal movements of the mind traveling along these timelines do considerable harm to the meditator. They are produced by attachment to what was experienced in a moment in the past, or to the expectations one nurtures about the future. But past and future are not the moment of expression of the self. The higher self acts in the present moment because it is the only moment that exists, and the higher self is the only real presence in this moment. All the rest are raw perceptions that have been resignified by the mind and become artificial presences in the subjective scene of the mind. The present is the time of the self. Its position, without any doubt, is in the first-person universe, where the mind sees the higher self.

The future or the past, by definition, contain everything that is not in the present, and that, therefore, can only be referred to in the third-person. They are times that only exist in the focus point of the object. And just as others should not be reference for the decisions of the higher self, past and future should not be reference for the perception of the present. These are only references for the mind to build the dreamlike setting in which the higher self enjoys its personality. One must free oneself from all dependence on past and future, as this dependence mistakenly removes the meditative focus from the present moment, immobilizing one's will and impairing meditation.

One must remove the past from meditative focus. This is achieved through unattachment to that which has passed, bearing in mind the fact that the subject is not defined by what has been accomplished in the past. The subject is just the higher self, found only in the present and the subject of the past is non-existent, just like the past itself, which is just a narrative. Present realization must be anchored in the meditator's authentic nature, only, and not in their resume or biography. The past, whether good or bad, serves only as a source for reflection, in the objective focus point.

The future should also be outside of meditative focus, as the mind cannot rely on fuzzy uncertainties. The future should become another source of reflection in the objective focus point, which helps to pave the path to be followed as an unknown present and not as a project built through reason. Only in this way, through unattachment from the past and future, is the meditator able to fully live their higher self.

Time delimits the power of the vāsanās but does not limit the liberating power of dhyānam, which destroys the disturbances of the activities of the mind. Through dhyānam, disturbed mental activities cease and the mind becomes ready to receive intuition from Puruṣa. As it is only possible to perceive Puruṣa experientially, in the present moment, this is the only moment available for those who wish to succeed in meditation. In yoga, meditation is not concerned with things that change, but with the transformation itself. Meditation seeks support from the greater 'self' who, despite being unchanging, is the only real cause of change. The transformations attributed to time, which characterize its uninterrupted march, affect only transitory material qualities – the guṇas. The transformations do not affect the imperishable and unchanging Puruṣa, who is not limited by time, but is the inner 'self' and 'guru' present in the inner space of the heart of each creature.

In the first chapter of the Yoga Sūtras, Patañjali says:

"Īśvara is a special Puruṣa (...), they are also the guru of the ancients

Mythical time is what converts the narrative into a gateway to the universe of Puruṣa, making words the glue that holds the mind's attention in the present time. Narrative mythical time is indeterminate time that, as it escapes both the limits of historical assertions and future speculations, ends up comfortably settling on the perpetuity of the present.

But is the present, in fact, everlasting? What is the true duration of the present? This question deserves a brief reflection. Turn your attention to the present and try to discover when the transition from the present to the past takes place. If you are in the present, how many seconds ago did the past begin? And also, assess how far ahead the future is from now.

If you think about it, you might come to the conclusion that no time separates the present from the past or the present from the future. Past and future extend, in opposite directions along the lines of time, from right now, not an instant more or less. The present is just the boundary between the before and after of now. It has no duration - strictly speaking, it does not exist. But the present is the only part of time accessible to consciousness, it is all that can be captured from first-person time, where meanings of Puruṣa are lodged and become the mythical foundations of the mind. The present does not exist, but it is always there, available, indestructible, eternal, alive. In contrast to the present, the past and future embrace everything that is perishable and guard all the limits of life, including the mystery of death - the final point of discourse.

In the Bhagavad Gītā, chapter 11 is called 'The Vision of Viśvarūpa (the universal form).' In this chapter, Kṛṣṇa reveals to Arjuna his true appearance as a universal form. At one point, Arjuna, frightened, compares Viśvarūpa's face to the devouring fire of time (*kālānala*). Is Kṛṣṇa, then, who presents himself as the indestructible higher self, the origin of time? The Gītā confirms that he is. It may seem paradoxical, for time is the foundation of the material transformations and raw material of mortality, but Kṛṣṇa himself presents himself in this way:

"Of the units of measurement, I am kāla (time)." [193] "I am time that

---

[192] Yoga Sūtras 1.24 and 1.26
[193] Bhagavad Gītā 10.30

produces destruction of the worlds."[194] "I am, in fact, unending time." [195]

Kṛṣṇa represents the higher self that gives foundation to existence and immortality but also identifies with time that determines the duration and destruction of all creatures. He also says, in the Gītā:

"I am the higher self, seated in the heart of all creatures (...). I am the beginning, middle and end of all creatures." [196]

The beginning (*ādi*) is the moment of birth, the middle (*madhyam*) is the duration of life (always in the present), and the end (*anta*) is the moment of death. Here is yet another reference to time connected to ātmā. Certainly, this reference is to first-person time, the present of the higher self that contrasts to the past and the future. The higher self, found in the eternal present, destroys with its fire the perishable world constructed by the mind. In the end, only this higher self exists. Only this higher self is beyond death. Only this higher self is the meditator.

The Kaṭha Upaniṣad says:

"A person (Puruṣa) the size of a thumb is in the middle of the higher self, the lord of the past (bhūtam) and the future (bhavyam), nothing is hidden from him. This is certainly him.

"A person the size of a thumb, as a light without smoke, lord of the past and the future, only he exists, today. Only he will be for certain tomorrow. This is certainly him." [197]

---

[194] Bhagavad Gītā 10.32
[195] Bhagavad Gītā 10.33
[196] Bhagavad Gītā 10.20
[197] Kaṭha Upaniṣad 4.1.12 and 4.1.13

20. Uttamapuruṣa and Power

From what we have seen so far, we can say that a meditative life is built with a mind governed by the quality of sattvam and is lived only in the first-person. It is easy to understand why Sanskrit culture calls the verbal first-person *'the supreme person'*: *'Uttamapuruṣa'*. The longer we remain in the condition of the first-person, the happier we become and the more meditative our mind becomes. But what does it mean to 'live a life in the first-person?'

It is relatively easy to live in the first-person, when these four recommendations are followed:

The first recommendation is to park oneself in the present. The past and future are useful references for a work schedule but are quite limiting when dealing with a project of life. Ask yourself, for example, "what do I want to do now?" or "what meaning does this moment have for me?" But do not let the mind construct a reply. Ignore the inner chatter of the mind and just try to see what appears in front of you, as a response to these questions. Be attentive and observe, without interfering, the thoughts that arise to your inner gaze through your intuition. Don't think about a response, just allow your intuition to be revealed.

The second recommendation for living life in the first-person is to look for the good in each situation, noting the qualities of others. This is an attitude that we all would like to see in the behavior of others. Everyone wants to be seen with 'good eyes', although they use the mind's imaginative eyes to enhance or diminish the qualities or defects of others and of situations involving others. Note that it's not about closing your eyes to what's bad, and avoiding reality, but always looking with eyes wide open. It is possible to see things the way they really are if you just don't allow yourself to become passively involved with whatever you see. By doing this, your meditation can happen fully.

The third recommendation is to let go of everything that is not related to your own nature. It is very common to make commitments and engage in actions inappropriately, causing conflicts with your personal nature. Such initiatives are motivated by attachment to goods, people, opinions, and values relevant to the lives of others. It is essential to free the mind from attachment to the values of others. This is why unattachment and discipline are presented by Patanjali as indispensable conditions for quality meditation.

The fourth recommendation for living in the first-person is to relax and enjoy life, with contentment. Relaxing the mind and body is good for one's well-being, because when the mind is tense, it is unable to properly adjust to Puruṣa. All tension originates in the mind, defensively resulting from fear or doubts about decisions that need to be made, or in relation to other people's reactions. Being alive is an experience that can be enjoyed much more intensely if you release your tensions. A relaxed life involves such things as taking breaks from work, processing stress completely, completion of assigned tasks (clearing backlogs), and contentment – whatever the outcome.

By heeding these four recommendations, the meditator will certainly help their mind to become lighter and will be more apt to enjoy life in the first-person. But knowing what needs to be done is not enough. An additional recommendation should be taken into consideration: *do whatever is appropriate and that depends on you to get done*. This recommendation requires us to mobilize our individual will, which is Puruṣa's inner voice of command within the mind. But if the mind is not cleansed of external interferences, Puruṣa's will may be overshadowed by a desire that finds any justification to get into the line of command. Knowing Puruṣa's will is the most important thing that can be known, but still, the mind moved by desire can be dragged away from it. Desire is the great enemy of Uttamapuruṣa, the enjoyer. Kṛṣṇa says to Arjuna, explaining this desire:

"Knowledge is obscured by this permanent enemy of the knower, who takes the form of desire, o Kaunteya, and is an insatiable fire. It is said that this fire lives in the senses, in the mind and in perceptive

intelligence. Through these, having obscured knowledge, (the desire) deceives the soul." [198]

Desire affects only the mind, moving it away from the sattvam condition, which is necessary for meditation to be successful. This is the main reason why the meditator needs to free their mind from the harmful effects of desire. But the mind, which builds a web connecting the higher self to the objective world, is also the foundation of consciousness. Desire distorts the mental image of the world by bringing impurities, inappropriate content, into the inner space of the mind. In order to do away with desire, and restore the purity of the mind, it is necessary to plunge into a state similar to unconsciousness, temporarily suspending the control of the mind over the sensory organs and the organs of action. Unconsciousness, however, is a frightening abyss for the mind, that needs sensory stimuli, information, to experience the comforting sensation of its importance and of its very existence.

Although it makes the mind dizzy, unconsciousness is the natural path leading to Puruṣa. This is why it is recommended that the meditator establish a firm foundation in the realm of the unconscious, for the higher self to settle in the heart (*Prājña*), as the actor that plays the role of Puruṣa within each individual. The role of this 'self in the heart' is to serve as a vehicle that gives voice to intuition (*prajñā*) emanating directly from Puruṣa. If the meditator assumes this heart's self as their own identity, desire loses hold and disappears. Hence the importance of the mind going through symbolic death (through unconsciousness) to achieve immortality, awakening the power of *vīrya*, the inner fearlessness of the hero (*vīra*).

The condition of the heroic mind is similar to the condition of a child's mind, amazed by the surrounding world. This condition is achieved by consciously discarding all the meanings that the mind has ever associated with the objects around it until the whole environment appears as an indistinct mass of unidentified stimuli. This is like what happens, for example, when one reads while sleepy; the words of the text are seen, but, although they are identified, they do not take on any meaning in the mind. After reaching this relaxed state, the mind is intentionally allowed to receive the flow of intuitive meanings from the higher self, so that the environment gains meanings that are not thought, but intuited by the mind.

---

[198] Bhagavad Gītā 3.39 and 3.40

This same result becomes possible also through sleep, the mind's natural path to find unconsciousness, in the realm of the heart's self. The exercise of adjusting the mind to a state of deep sleep, in which desire becomes meaningless and disappears, is called *nidrāyoga* or *yoganidrā*. This adjustment of the sleep state offers support to the meditator, as it strengthens their self-confidence and provides sustainability (*dhāraṇam*) to meditation. As a mythical character, the goddess *Yoganidrā*, sometimes called *Yogamāyā*, also manifests in the form of intuition enjoyed by the higher self in the deep sleep of unconsciousness. The mind is unable to register its experience with Yoganidrā, which is only successfully enjoyed by the higher self. This goddess personifies Brahma's sleep in the dissolution of the universe into a state in which only the higher self exists. According to Haṭha Yoga Pradīpikā, in order to achieve the benefits of yoganidrā, the inner path called 'khecarī mudrā' must be followed:

> *"One should practice Khecarī as much as needed to attain the condition of yoganidrā. The (final) moment never arrives for those who reach yoganidrā."* [199]

The word *khecarī* is the feminine form of *khecara*, an adjective that means 'flying' or 'moving in space.' It is composed from two words: '*khe*' (locative inflection of '*kham* - 'space') and '*cara*' ('walking'). Kham is the inner space of the mind, made up entirely of narrative thoughts of mythical nature. When Puruṣa's attention moves into this subjective mythical space, isolating itself from interferences of the natural world, the mind reaches the condition of yoganidrā. This is when the purified formative *tattvāni* (the three principles: *buddhi*, *ahaṁkāra* and *manas*) merge with the true nature of the meditator (their *svadharma*) in a transparent way. And so, the mind is enlightened with the understanding that comes from the higher self, Puruṣa. Vasiṣṭha says to the prince Rāma:

> *"The pure components of cittam find each other. Waters of the same nature flow united, but not the polluted. The purity of cittam actually brings about the ability to illuminate (with the light of understanding) a subjective perception (abhūta). Unification of appearance takes place quickly, due to the purity (of the mind). Due to this (understanding) that has been awakened, supreme integration (with Puruṣa) is found through adjustment of the tanmātras."* [200]

---

[199] Haṭha Yoga Pradīpikā 4.49
[200] Yoga Vāsiṣṭha 4.17.30 and 4.17.31

Tanmātras are those components of nature that demarcate the limits of what is possible to know in the universe. They act on the functioning of the organs of action and perception, regulating each creature's capacity for action and cognition. When they are adjusted to the understanding of Puruṣa, the capacities of the mind are amplified and their reach expands to encompass even unconscious knowledge. The poetic image of pure waters, which merge with the current, reveals how the ancient sages tried to solve the greatest mystery that hovers over the workings of the mind: the mechanism that makes possible the exchange of information between two apparently incompatible perspectives, that of the higher self (first-person) and the mind (third-person).

The explanation that appears in that verse uses an analogy of movement of information that passes through the mind, equating it to the movement of water currents. Pure waters that move together and impure waters that don't mix together. "*The pure components of cittam find each other*" like waters of the same purity that "*flow united.*" The components of cittam are *buddhi*, *ahaṁkāra* and *manas*, which can only be considered pure when a filter ('*pavitram*') - the higher self [201] - has removed their impurities - external interferences related to the power of desire over the mind. It is important to remember here that the flowing waters of a river (nadī) is an image used in the Hindu tradition to describe the movement of prāṇa through tubular channels called nāḍīs, which connect to the mind like rivers that flow into the sea. The fine mesh built by these tubular conduits, as such, is a part of the structure of the subtle or subjective body, that is, of the mind.

According to traditional imagery, impurities in the mind are deposited in certain points in this tubular network, just as happens with impurities that are thrown into rivers. They accumulate and become obstacles to the free flow of information in the mind. As a result, personal intelligence, which travels through the tubular network in the form of prāṇa, is impaired. With these obstructions, the light of Puruṣa's knowledge is hidden, covered by impurities. Patañjali states that the impurities are removed through the practice of prāṇāyāma. He says:

"The concealment of the light (of Puruṣa) is destroyed (through the practice of prāṇāyāma)." [202]

---

201 See in the Bhagavad Gītā 9.17 – "*... I am the purifier (pavitram)...*"
202 Yoga Sūtras 2.52

This phrase is part of the passage in which Patañjali explains prāṇāyāma. The light to which he refers is understanding, the main source of the powers of the mind. Vyāsa, in his commentary on this sūtra, cites a clarifying phrase, without revealing its author:

"(...) It is said: there are no tapas superior to prāṇāyāma. From prāṇāyāma comes the purification of impurities and the light of knowledge." [203]

Tapas, despite often being remembered for scenes of mortification or self-inflicted suffering, is associated in yogic literature with subjective acts of purification of the mind. Hence, prāṇāyāma is considered to be a form of tapas, that is, a ritual to remove impurities. This same opinion is expressed in the literature of the Nāthas, produced some centuries after Vyāsa's time. See, for example, what the Haṭha Yoga Pradīpikā says in its chapter on prāṇāyāma:

"Only through prāṇāyāmas are all impurities removed. None of the ācāryas, however, approves any other action (aimed at purification)." [204]

As stated previously in chapter 13, prāṇāyāma is control over the movement of meanings and their application to information brought into the subjective space of the mind from the external world. If this information is correctly filtered, that is, aligned with the higher self, all of the knowledge that emerges from it would be true, according to the Hindu theory of meditation. Arising from the deep darkness of unconsciousness, the light of understanding reveals only the truth. As a brāhmin states in the Mahābhāratam:

"Brahma is the truth, tapas is the truth and the Creator (Prajāpati) is only truth. From the truth, creatures are produced. The truth is the real world." [205]

The inclusion of tapas in this verse of the epic reveals the importance that these acts of purification have gained in the Sanskrit tradition of meditation. The statement that *"tapas is the truth"* suggests that purification of the mind results from a vow of allegiance to the truth. The quote cited by Vyāsa stating that *"there is no tapas superior to prāṇāyāma"*, points to the

---

[203] Yoga Sūtra Bhāṣya 2.52
[204] Haṭha Yoga Pradīpikā 2.37
[205] Mahābhāratam 14.35.34

belief that purification happens as consequence of the free movement of the breath of Puruṣa in the subtle body of the meditator. When the mind is freed of falsities, of impurities, it becomes, to some extent, equal to Puruṣa. Freed by the commitment made to the truth, the mind enjoys a state of permanent contentment and happiness.

We previously discussed in chapter 18 the power of happiness; whereby the mind is no longer an obstacle to samādhi and actually becomes a direct path to it. There are many powers that arise when one practices meditation. Several of them are mentioned in the third chapter of the Yoga Sūtras, starting with verse 3.16. They are skills and knowledge that elevate the yogi to a higher level of resources to live one's life. The chapter of the Sūtras that discusses this topic is called Vibhūti Pāda - the Chapter of Power, where Patañjali repeatedly uses the following formula:

Meditation focused (saṁyama) on certain objects will result in the ability to obtain certain kinds of *knowledge*. And meditation focused on other objects will result in the manifestation of abilities to carry out *extraordinary actions*. The powers described there, in the form of abilities to obtain knowledge or perform actions, show consistency with the theoretical postulations of the Sāṁkhya philosophy. Extraordinary knowledge gained with the help of the organs of perception (*buddhīndriyāni*) that have become hypersensitive through the practice of meditation; and extraordinary action is achieved with the help of organs of action (*karmendriyāni*), sensitized by meditation.

There is a caveat here. The only enjoyer of these powers is Puruṣa, the personhood of the higher self. These powers should serve the purpose of Puruṣa, and not the mind - which is only an instrument for Puruṣa.

Puruṣa or Brahma is also the higher self, the source from which all powers related to our relationship with material nature arise. From the point of view of the upaniṣads, these powers, which enable one to perform actions or to gain knowledge, can be reduced to two great feminine attributes of Brahma. In the upaniṣads, each of these attributes is presented as a force (śakti) specialized in dynamizing part of the activities of the mind. *Kriyāśakti* mobilizes the activities of the mind connected to the five organs of action and *jñānaśakti* or *dhīśakti* mobilizes the activities of the mind connected to the five organs of perception. However, no force connected with the activities of the mind related to manas, the 'eleventh organ' of the subjective body, is attributed to Brahma. Manas occupies a position of command over all of the other organs and should be provided with a force corresponding to its status as Īśvara. This force seems to be absent, or simply is not mentioned by its own name in the older upaniṣads.

There are yogic texts, such as Valmīki's Yoga Vāsiṣṭha, which perhaps attempt to cover this concept under the name 'saṁkalpa' (imagination or intention). But saṁkalpa is a creative activity of the mind, not exactly a force. The characteristic of the force that we are looking for is the same as that of manas: to connect and disconnect objects and concepts. It corresponds more precisely to the 'desire-aversion' pair, which appears a few times in the epic Mahābhāratam as 'icchā-dveṣa.' The same pair appears in the Yoga Sūtras as one of the disturbances of the mind, as *rāga-dveṣa*.[206] The word 'icchā', used several times in the epic, means both 'will' and 'desire' and can be used to identify the force of Brahma linked to manas. It comes from the verbal root 'iṣ' ('to want'), from which the term 'Īśvara' ('lord' or 'commander') is also constructed.

That force that is missing from the upaniṣads related to the power of manas, could be identified by the word *icchāśakti* which does in deed appear in yogic literature. The use of 'icchāśakti' is found in the tantric literature of Kashmir, used in a trio with the expressions *jñānaśakti* and *kriyāśakti*. It is found in the composite form 'icchā-jñāna-kriyā-śakti' in the Tantrāloka (5.55-56) by Abhinavagupta, a Shaivite philosopher from the second half of the 10th century. It also appears in the form 'icchāśakti' in the commentary on the Tantrāloka Viveka (5.91) by Rājānaka Jayaratha, a Kashmir poet, from the 12th century. It seems, then, that *icchāśakti* is the right word to identify the force of Brahma connected to the principle manas.

The correct use of this force frees the mind and allows for meditation to occur and disturbances to be removed from its field of action. This is why it is so important to cultivate will, which is the benign side of desire. This power of will, a gift of Uttamapuruṣa, the first-person, arises only when the mind, free from any external interference, guides all its activities by the truth alone.

---

[206] Yoga Sūtras 2.7 and 2.8

सत्यमेव जयते

'Only the truth wins'

(Muṇḍaka Upaniṣad 3.1.6)

Bibliography

BARBOSA, Carlos E. G.. Os Yoga Sutras de Patanjali [translation and commentary]. São Paulo: Mantra, 2015.

BARBOSA, Carlos E. G.. Bhagavad Gītā [translation and commentary]. São Paulo: Mantra, 2018.

Chalmers, David J. The Character of Consciousness (Philosophy of Mind). Oxford University Press. Kindle edition.

Chalmers, David J. The Conscious Mind (Philosophy of Mind). Oxford University Press. Kindle edition.

DAMASIO, Antonio. Self Comes to Mind. 2010. New York, Knopf Doubleday Publishing Group. Kindle edition.

Dennett, Daniel C. Consciousness Explained. 2017, New York, Little, Brown and Company, Kindle Edition.

Goleman, Daniel. Emotional Intelligence: Why It Can Matter More Than IQ. Random House Publishing Group. Kindle edition.

Goleman, Daniel. The Science of Meditation: How to Change Your Brain, Mind and Body. Penguin Books Ltd. Kindle edition.

Kant, Immanuel. Critique of Pure Reason (Annotated). Kindle edition.

KIM, Jaegwon. Philosophy of Mind. Taylor and Francis. Kindle edition.

KUVALAYANANDA, Swami. Pranayama. São Paulo: Phorte, 2008.

Paz, Octavio. The Bow and the Lyre (Texas Pan American Series). Austin: University of Texas Press. Kindle edition.

ROGERS, Carl R. On Becoming a Person. Little, Brown Book Group. Kindle edition.

SAUSSURE, Ferdinand de. Cours de Linguistique Générale [annoté] (French Edition). Philaubooks. Kindle edition.

VIVEKANANDA, Swami. Complete Works of Swami Vivekananda, volume 1, "Raja Yoga." Kindle edition.

Sources of the original texts in Sanskrit

Bhagavad Gītā – *Srīmad Bhagavad Gītā Bhāṣya of Sri Saṁkarācārya.* Madras. Sri Ramakrishna Math. 2008.

> – Includes: Bhagavad Gītā Bhāṣya

Haṭha Yoga Pradīpikā – *The Haṭhayogapradīpikā.* Delhi. Chaukhamba Sanskrit Pratishthan. 2003.

Mahābhāratam

> – BORI critique edition – Vishnu S. Sukthankar & S.K. Belvalkar: *The Mahābhārata.* Poona. Bhandarkar Oriental Research Institute (BORI). 1959.

> – Parimal Edition – M.N.Dutt: *Mahābhārata.* Delhi. Parimal Publications. 2018.

Ṛg Veda - *Ṛgveda Saṁhitā.* Delhi. Chaukhamba Sanskrit Pratishthan.

Sarva Darśana Saṁgraha – *Sarvadarśanasaṁgraha.* Mumbai. Prācya vidyā Saṁśodhana Mandira. 1924. [*This text is usually attributed to Mādhavācārya Vidyāraṇya, but the edition that we used as reference identifies the author the more famous brother of Vidyāraṇya, named Sāyaṇa Mādhavācārya. The fact is that the two of them wrote some works together, and this is one of those.*]

Sāṁkhya Kārikā – *The Sāṁkhya-Kārikā.* Poona. Oriental Book Agency. 1933.

> – Includes: Sāṁkhya Kārikā Bhāṣya

Siddha Siddhānta Paddhati – *Siddhasiddhāntapaddhati.* Lonavla. The Lonavla Yoga Institute (India). 2016.

Tantrāloka – *The Tantrāloka of Abhinava Gupta (with commentary by Rājānaka Jayaratha).* Allahabad. The Research Department Jammu & Kashmir State. 1918.

> – Includes: Tantrāloka Viveka

Upaniṣadas – *112 Upaniṣads*. Delhi. Parimal Publications. 2006.

- Includes: Aitareya Upaniṣad, Brahma Bindu Upaniṣad, Bṛhadāraṇyaka Upaniṣad, Chāndogya Upaniṣad, Īśāvāsya Upaniṣad, Kaivalya Upaniṣad, Kaṭha Upaniṣad, Kauṣītaki Brāhmaṇopaniṣad, Maitreyyupaniṣad, Māṇḍukya Upaniṣad, Muṇḍaka Upaniṣad, Praśna Upaniṣad, Śvetāśvatara Upaniṣad, Taittirīya Upaniṣad, Tejobindu Upaniṣad.

Yoga Sūtras – *Yogasūtrabhāṣyavivaraṇa of Śaṅkara*. New Delhi. Munshiram Manoharlal Publishers. 2010.

– Includes: Yoga Sūtra Bhāṣya and Yoga Sūtra Bhāṣya Vivaraṇa.

Yoga Vāsiṣṭha – *The Yoga Vāsiṣṭha of Vālmīki*. Delhi. Parimal Publications. 2005.

The Author

Carlos Eduardo Gonzales Barbosa

Instructor of Sanskrit Culture of Yoga

Brazilian, Carlos resides in Florianópolis, Santa Catarina.

Carlos Eduardo Gonzales Barbosa began studying Indian culture in 1972. He studied Sanskrit at the University of São Paulo (1979-1982) and has been teaching Sanskrit language and culture since 1982, with a focus on yoga. Carlos taught as part of the teacher training program of the *Centro de Estudos de Yoga Narayana* (São Paulo) for 28 years. He is the co-author of the book *"O Livro de Ouro do Yoga"* (Ediouro, São Paulo, 2007) and author of the book *"A Meditação dos Yoguis"* (Traço, São Paulo, 2011). He translated the Yoga Sutras (Mantra, São Paulo, 2015), the Bhagavad Gita (Mantra, São Paulo, 2018), and the Kaṭha Upaniṣad (Yogaforum, Florianopolis, 2022) from Sanskrit to Portuguese.

At the moment, he is dedicated to the dissemination of foundational Sanskrit texts for yoga through distance learning and books. He teaches online courses as part of the yoga teacher training of IYTA-Brasil (International Yoga Teachers Association). He is the editor of the website Sanskritforum.org, where he maintains online courses in his specialty.